THEN AND THERE SERIES
GENERAL EDITOR
MARJORIE REEVES M.A. PH.D.

Holland in the Time of Rembrandt

HEATHER CUBITT

D1613236

LONGMAN

LONGMAN GROUP LIMITED
London

*Associated companies, branches and representatives
throughout the world*

© *Longman Group Ltd 1971*
*All rights reserved. No part of this publication
may be reproduced, stored in a retrieval system
or transmitted in any form or by any means,
electronic, mechanical, photocopying, recording
or otherwise, without the prior permission
of the Copyright owner.*

First published 1971

ISBN 0 582 20522 0

*Photoset in Malta by St Paul's Press Ltd
Printed in Hong Kong by
Dai Nippon Printing Co., (International) Ltd.*

Acknowledgements

British Museum, pages 11, 31, 64 and 71; Fitzwilliam Museum, Cambridge, page 79; Foundation
Johan Maurits van Nassau, the Hague, page 50; Frans Halsmuseum, Haarlem, pages 32, 43, 57, 58
left and *right*, 60, 61 and 102; Kunsthistoreschen Museum, Vienna, page 37; National Gallery, pages
15, 19, 23, 40 and 48; National Maritime Museum, pages 7, 66, 81, 85 and 87; National Portrait
Gallery, page 2; Rijksmuseum, Amsterdam, pages 9, 12, 18, 22, 26, 28, 29, 34, 69, 74, 76, 83, 89, 91,
93, 96 and 101; Staatliche Museum, Berlin, page 16; Stadelschen Kunstinstituts, Frankfurt, page 41;
Duke of Sutherland, page 52; Christopher Lloyd, *Ships and Seamen*, Weidenfeld and Nicolson, pages
7, 64 and 71.

Contents

To The Reader

Holland was one of the greatest countries in seventeenth-century Europe: great not in wars, in which she was sometimes defeated; nor in size: there were only two million people in Holland (England had three times as many, France ten times as many). Holland was great in what her people achieved.

At a time when many other European countries, and those in the East, were often governed harshly by strong kings or emperors, Holland was ruled by her leading citizens, and her people had a say in their affairs. She was one of the first countries to move towards a more *democratic* government. Catholics, Protestants and Jews could worship in their different ways with some freedom in Holland, while in many lands elsewhere groups of these people were still being badly treated. Refugees and exiles from other countries might find a welcome in her busy cities.

Holland was securing mastery of the sea, both in draining it from her land, and in sending her sailors exploring the four quarters of the globe. Dutchmen settled in distant lands, and controlled much of the trade of Europe, and Dutch artists of great skill could be found in every leading city.

The Dutch fought a bitter war to win their independence from Philip II of Spain who ruled them in the sixteenth century. Only the seven northern provinces (known as the United Provinces) succeeded, and modern Holland was created as an independent country. Modern Belgium, as the southern provinces came to be, did not gain its freedom for two more centuries. This book will tell you more about why the seventeenth century was indeed 'the Golden Age of Holland'.

Words printed in *italics* in the text are explained in the glossary, p. 107.

1 Sir William Temple Arrives in the Netherlands

The year was 1668, and the English ship carrying the English ambassador Sir William Temple, his family and attendants, sailed into the harbour at Rotterdam. For many of them it was a first visit to the Netherlands, but for Temple it was a return to a country he knew well and greatly admired.

Sir William had had a sound education in Latin and Greek at the grammar school at Bishop's Stortford, and at Emmanuel College, Cambridge, and he came from a well connected family owning considerable estates in Ireland. His father, thinking he would be well suited to a career in the foreign service, had sent him abroad to travel widely, and to improve his languages. So the young man had visited Germany, France and the Netherlands, and soon spoke Spanish, French and Dutch well. He had great charm, and a tactful manner, and showed all the makings of a good *diplomat*.

On one of these holidays, when he was twenty, he had fallen passionately in love with Dorothy Osborne who, after many hardships, was to become his wife. She and her brother Robin were visiting the Isle of Wight on their way to France, and became friendly with William. Robin had foolishly scratched with a diamond on the windowpane of their inn an offensive remark against the government, and the whole party of young people had been arrested and brought before the governor. Dorothy had shown resourcefulness and cool courage, and had taken the entire blame for the affair, so that the gallant governor set them free. William Temple became her devoted admirer.

Both Sir John Temple and Sir Peter Osborne opposed the marriage of their children, thinking that better matches might

*Sir William Temple, English Ambassador in Holland (Peter Lely)**

be arranged, and it was nearly seven years before William and Dorothy could finally wed. For two years they exchanged weekly love letters, sending them secretly by trusted friends. William's

2　*The name in brackets after some of the pictures is that of the artist.

letters, apart from one, have been lost, but we still have Dorothy's charming, frank and witty replies. She had a great gift of expressing her moods and feelings, was generous, and devoted to William. According to the custom of the day, they exchanged locks of hair, and golden rings as a pledge of their love. William was full of jealousy when he heard that no fewer than six suitors were hoping for her hand. One of them was a formidable rival: Henry Cromwell, son of Oliver Cromwell, then ruling England. Henry was a handsome fellow who sent her a delightful present of two fine greyhounds which almost won Dorothy's heart.

Finally, after further family opposition, and Dorothy's recovery from a severe attack of smallpox, she and William were quietly married on Christmas Day in 1654. Dorothy accompanied William to his post as ambassador abroad, and she became greatly loved by people in the Netherlands. She showed great tact and courage on many occasions, and was also able to persuade the English government to pay William his long overdue salary, for Charles II treated his ambassador at the Hague quite shamefully in this respect.

William's sister Martha also went with the family to Holland. Her husband, Sir Thomas Gifford, had died a month after her marriage, and she spent the rest of her life with the Temples. She wrote, with sisterly frankness, a life of her brother. She describes him as tall and handsome, with fine dark, curly hair, and lively grey eyes. He loved music, and as a young man was very active, being particularly fond of tennis, riding and walking. William was warm-hearted, and had great charm. He was witty and entertaining in conversation, humane and kindly, and took great pleasure in making others happy. One of his weaknesses was that he was somewhat lazy, although he would make a determined effort to do something if it were really important. His mood could change quickly, too, from being gay to being sad and dejected, and he seemed to be very much affected by the fogs and damp of Holland.

William was a very honest person, and people usually trusted him completely. This was very valuable for an ambassador. However, he often imagined that others were equally honest, 3

The seven United provinces

and was sometimes bitterly disappointed when they failed him. He was not ambitious to become great or wealthy, and although his home was full of beautiful pictures and statues, he led a very

4

simple life, wore plain clothes, employed few servants, and enjoyed the company of his family and friends more than that of the great men of the English court.

Because he delighted in his garden, had simple tastes and loved freedom and *moderation*, William was much at home in Holland. He made many friends there, and believed strongly that the English and Dutch peoples had much in common, and should work together. He thought the great enemy of them both was France which was becoming strong and aggressive in the seventeenth century.

Earlier in 1668 William had had his greatest triumph in arranging a friendly treaty between England, Holland and Sweden called the Triple Alliance. William had been persistent and energetic, and had long talks with the Dutch statesman De Witt, whom he found frank and direct. They worked hard for five days and nights to improve the relations between the two countries, and when the treaty was signed, it was received enthusiastically in Holland. It was equally popular in England with most people, and Pepys, the English diaryist, wrote that it pleased everybody and was the first good thing the king had done.

On his return to England William wrote a detailed book called 'Observations on the United Provinces of the Netherlands', published in 1673. In it he described his ideas about the country, the people, and why they were great and prosperous. You will find some of his thoughts, and those of other visitors to Holland in the later chapters of this book.

2 First Impressions of Seventeenth century Amsterdam

'Here resided the soul of the Dutch state', wrote the poet Vondel of Amsterdam. For Amsterdam with its 140,000 people was bigger by far than any other city in Holland, and nine times bigger than the attractive and residential centre of government, The Hague. It was the hub of trade and business of the whole country, not only of the state of Holland, and English visitors, like all foreigners, were greatly impressed by its huge size and magnificent buildings.

Like many other towns, it was originally surrounded by a wall with defensive towers at intervals, but by the seventeenth century there was no need for these, and the wall had been gradually pulled down to allow new houses to be developed on the outskirts. Much of the city was built on marshy soil by the river Amstel, and many of the houses were constructed on stout wood pilings as a strong foundation against the treacherous *subsoil*.

Numerous canals encircled the city, and alongside these were the quays and warehouses, and in the residential areas, the gracious houses of the more wealthy merchants. The fine Amsterdam Exchange, built early in the century, where bargains and contracts were signed, and deals completed in the busy morning hours, was built above a canal, and large ships could sail under its vaults after lowering their masts. People tied their boats to mooring posts by the canal at the foot of steps leading to their houses, and went to work by water. If they were walking through the town, they accepted as a matter of course that they would cross innumerable canals by little wooden foot-bridges. They might have to wait a few moments while part of the bridge

17th century Amsterdam, a forest of masts

was raised to allow a tall masted ship to pass by, and then the bridge would be lowered again. Stalls with fruit, fish, cheese and vegetables were to be found by the canal sides, their wares being supplied by the numerous barges that slowly passed up and down the waterways, some wide, some so narrow that you could touch the walls of the buildings on either side as you sailed by.

Along the side of the canal was usually a well paved road of rough stone or tightly packed hard brick, with a small footpath for pedestrians. Most of the city roads were paved in this way, and they appeared remarkably clean to most foreigners, used to muddy tracks or uneven cobbles with a dirty channel in the middle, full of filthy water and rubbish. William Temple thought that the extreme moisture of the air in Holland encouraged the people to pave their streets, and build long stone *causeways* between their towns, or the soil would be muddy and impassable. He was much impressed by the Dutch housewives' passion for keeping their houses spotless. Everywhere they could be seen with brushes and pails, washing the steps leading to the front door, sweeping the brick paving stones of their courtyards, or polishing brass handles and door knockers. Woe betide thoughtless husbands who brought the slightest speck of dirt into the house! They usually left their dusty shoes on the mat in the hall, and tiptoed into the main room in their stockinged feet.

On one occasion, while visiting the mayor of Amsterdam, William Temple, who had a nasty cough, spat on the floor. This disgusting habit was accepted as normal practice in England at the time. The shocked Dutch host immediately ordered his maidservant to fetch a cloth to wipe the floor, and soundly rebuked the offending visitor, telling him that if he had not been the English ambassador and an honoured guest, his wife would certainly have instantly thrown him out of the house.

Alongside the more important canals stood the fine brick houses of the wealthy merchants. They were a mellow, yellowish red colour, often two or three storeys high, and gave the impression of being tall and narrow. Below street level, and reached by two or three steps, was the basement room where

8

the merchants' goods could be stored, and this part of the house might be tarred to keep out the damp. Other steps from the road led up to the strong front door, with its imposing brass or iron door knocker. On either side of the door were large casement windows, gay with brightly painted red, green, brown or white shutters. In rather less well-to-do houses, the front door was often divided into two sections, rather like a stable door. The lower half only might be closed, a useful arrangement which prevented the toddlers from straying out of doors and falling into the canals. On pleasant summer days the owners could be seen leaning out of the door, chatting to their neighbours, and there was the added advantage that more light could be let into the inner rooms.

Above the windows on the ground floor and running all

The old town hall in Amsterdam. Notice the shops and shuttered windows (Pieter Saenredam)

along the outside of the house there was often a wooden canopy which provided shade or some protection from sudden showers. Below this you could often see the housewife sitting on a bench making lace, or the father smoking his clay pipe, or children playing marbles. In some ways, however, it was the skyline and roofs of prosperous Dutch houses that were of the greatest interest. Some had steeply pitched *gables*, others elaborate scrolls and designs in stone. The attic was often a loft used for storing merchandise, and on the outside wall of the upper storey, instead of a window there might be a high door, and a pulley and ropes for hoisting cheeses, bales of cloth or other goods from the street below.

The brightly painted shutters, barrels, carts, and boats gave the streets and canals a gay and pleasant appearance, and added to these were the splendidly painted shop signs, done by local artists. They hung outside traders' shops, showing by a picture of an oven, a clay pipe or a red, white and blue striped pole, whether the shop was a baker's or a smoke room or a surgeon's shop. As elsewhere, people following the same trade tended to live in the same street, so that a housewife passing down Fishmongers' Row or Bakers' Lane could compare prices and choose from a number of shops. Many of the craftsmen, too, were still organised in *guilds* for their different trades. The master craftsman trained his *apprentices* carefully in the art of his trade, and officials laid down the hours of work, and prices and regulations affecting quality and sale.

In the poorer parts of the town, especially nearer the docks, conditions were not so pleasant. Here the old wooden houses, with their overhanging eaves cutting out much of the sunlight from the narrow, unpaved streets, had not yet been pulled down. There was much squalor, unemployment, and over-crowding, and with the growing population, many of the poorer people lived in wretched partitioned houses, whole families being crowded into one or two rooms. The danger of fire was much greater here, and although there were regulations laying down that citizens should have ladders and buckets in readiness to deal with outbreaks, these did not prevent frequent

FORUM AMSTELODAMENSE. DEN DAM. *Dijs* VOCANT.

A busy scene outside the fine new town hall and weigh-house. It shows the wealth of 17th century Amsterdam

A typical 17th century Dutch street (Vermeer)

fires from adding to the miseries of the poorer inhabitants who
lost their pitiful dwellings in these disasters.

Usually the city gave an impression of bustle and activity,

especially with the noise on the streets. Well-to-do people now travelled in gaily painted coaches which caused much confusion in the narrow streets. There was a well organised 'taxi' service in the city centre where people could ring a bell for service, and a number of coachmen, waiting nearby with their horses and vehicles, would come running up. They had a quaint custom of throwing a dice, and the 'lucky' coachman had the right to transport the visitor to his destination. Foreigners were also intrigued by the horsedrawn sledges moving through the streets of Amsterdam on greased runners. They carried goods of all kinds, and some had brightly painted tops constructed like carriages to carry passengers.

At night, the city was comparatively quiet, and few citizens ventured far. There were some candles and oil lamps in horn lanterns at street corners, and hanging above inns, but, as in most cities, the streets were dark, and there was the hazard of falling into a canal or being attacked by a robber lurking in the shadows. Any traveller at night who moved about without a lantern was suspected of being up to some mischief. At 10 p.m. a roll of drums heralded the arrival of the civic guard, a group of soldiers, armed with pikes, who with the night watchmen patrolled the city with dogs, and dealt with drunkards and thieves. But they often spent more time in drinking and gossiping in the guardroom in one of the old city towers than in wandering around the gloomy streets, and all self-respecting citizens would have returned to their homes long before midnight.

Coat of Arms of Amsterdam

3 The Dutch at Home

Vrouw Lysbeth Cuyper and her husband Pieter, a prosperous bookseller and printer, lived in a pleasant town house in Amsterdam overlooking one of the main canals. She was placid and attractive, with a rosy complexion and fair hair, and rather plump, like many Dutch women. Her home was spotlessly kept, with the help of her homely maidservant Judith, who had been with the household for years and was treated like one of the family.

The front door of the house opened into a well scrubbed entrance hall with three carefully arranged chairs. Here Pieter Cuyper sometimes went for a smoke, or conducted business with his friends. Beyond were a number of small rooms of somewhat confused arrangement, a steep narrow-stepped staircase leading to the upper ones, and a ladder to the loft. The Cuyper family's main living room had an attractive floor, patterned with blue and white tiles, and they had coloured tiles in some of the other rooms, although upstairs there were rough wooden floor boards. If there was company coming Vrouw Cuyper might put down, specially for the occasion, a little rush mat imported from Spain, or a small Turkish rug, but usually she preferred her clean coloured tiles. Judith scrubbed them daily, and when she had finished these, scrubbed the courtyard brickwork too.

The ceiling had open beams from which hung a wooden birdcage containing the family's pet parrot, and a little paper crown, somewhat faded with age, which Lysbeth had kept for sentimental reasons ever since she had worn it on her wedding day. Pictures of country scenes, maps of the Indies, and a little

A Dutch interior with its clean tiled floor (P. de Hooch, The Card Players*)*

gilded mirror Pieter had bought on a recent visit to France decorated the whitewashed walls.

Lysbeth's furniture was scanty, but beautifully kept, and smelling of fresh beeswax polish. In the living room was a folding gatelegged table and high backed chairs, several covered with leather or red coloured velvet fastened by shining copper nails, also a much valued *harpsichord*, and two large cupboards. One contained fine blue and white china, the other, sweet with the smell of lavender, held her closely guarded linen store – dozens of bonnets and caps, her own and her husband's fine lace collars, carefully folded sheets, pillowcases and napkins, many of which were inherited from her mother and grandmother.

Her bedroom upstairs, apart from its chair and a little washing stand, holding its basin and jug, was mostly filled by her much prized modern four-poster bed. It was entered by ornamental steps, and complete with splendid green and gold *damask* curtains and comfortable pillows, feather mat-

A Dutch living-room. Notice the high-backed chair, thick table cloth and attractive window (Vermeer, Herr and Dame beim Wein*)*

tress and coverlet. Lysbeth was especially proud of this bed; her children and many of her friends still slept in the traditional homely boxbeds built into one wall of the living room.

The chimes of the church clock, and the watchman's rattle and husky voice indicated that it was five o'clock. Sounds of shutters being fastened back by neighbours across the street reminded the family that it was time to rise. Already many craftsmen would be at work – dyers, and weavers, and smiths beating in their forges, milkmen and bakers on their rounds. Lysbeth had folded neatly in readiness on a chair the clothes she and her husband would require for the day; and put out a dark wig on a wigstand for Pieter (although sometimes he wore his own hair long) and her big white starched cap with flaps extending to the shoulder, which she would wear all day. There were freshly starched collars for them both. She and her husband had abandoned *ruffs* as rather old fashioned, but Lysbeth's old mother was still wearing them, and the traditional little chain round her waist, dangling with scissors, keys, knives and needles.

Foreigners thought the Dutch wore a large number of clothes, but this was perhaps necessary because their houses were not very well warmed. Pieter had a thick waistcoat, and his breeches were either baggy from waist to knee, or rather close-fitting, and decorated with French-style knots and bows. He had knitted stockings and wide-topped boots with turned down tops, or dark shoes fastened with a rosette. In the street Pieter wore a wide-brimmed floppy hat or a kind of top hat, and a cloak, but no overcoat.

He was most comfortable at home or in the office in his loose dressing robe, worn by nearly everyone. It was lined with fur or velvet and spread to his feet. Lysbeth had layers of petticoats, a warm skirt, decorated bodice, and a large number of white, black and violet aprons trimmed with lace. Both she and her husband preferred the dark fashionable colours, violet, black and dark brown, to those of a brighter hue.

At six o'clock, after some hasty washing, Lysbeth's large family, including Judith, were ready for breakfast, all standing

17

A Dutch kitchen maid (Vermeer)

behind their chairs while Pieter said grace. The men having replaced the hats they had removed for prayers, the meal began. There was little talk, and the smaller children were completely silent, while all consumed game and meat pies, bread and cheese, washed down by beer and milk.

After breakfast, Pieter departed for his shop, and Lysbeth was left to manage her household. She and Judith put on cloaks, and scarves, knotted under the chin. They had many battered *pewter* dishes and tankards to take to the pewterer to be remoulded and mended, for pewter was easily broken. Then

Lady and maid in a courtyard near the pump (P. de Hooch)

they made a trip to the fruit and vegetable market near the Weights and Measures office, and returned with their straw baskets laden with carrots, onions, cabbages and peas. After this much time was spent in the kitchen with its huge hearth above which hung a number of copper and pewter kitchen pots. On the wall was a salt box, and an *hourglass*, the only way of telling the time the household possessed. Water had to be collected in buckets from the pump in the courtyard outside, and washing was done in a large stone sink which was drained through a pipe into the yard.

Lysbeth worked hard preparing meals, for the family was fond of food. For lunch there was vegetable soup, probably a dish of fish (herrings, eels and cod were plentiful), salad, fruit and rice pudding, a favourite sweet. At 3 p.m. Lysbeth contented herself with a bread and cheese snack on her own, or occasionally had a fashionable tea or chocolate party with her women friends in the garden. They gossiped, and consumed delicious fancy cakes (filled with mixtures of cream, cinnamon, sugar and beaten egg) and biscuits flavoured with marzipan, cherries, raisins and dried fruit. If there was an opportunity she might spend some time in her small, trim garden with its formal beds of lilies, irises and roses, and its pear and apple trees. She grew cabbages, peas, turnips, onions and lettuces, but never enough for the family needs.

The Cuypers' eldest son Frans was seldom at home. He had lodgings in Leyden, was a successful student studying law at the university, and, through influential friends, hoped soon to obtain a good job at The Hague. He was not much interested in his father's printing presses, and the bales of paper, sea-charts, maps and bindings of glued leather stored in his workshop. More concerned with the printing were Pieter Cuyper's three apprentices. They lived with the household, and slept in the attic, their fathers having paid large fees for their training in the printing and publishing business. At first they had done little but run errands, sharpen quill pens, and make book entries, but after two years they now knew more about setting type, and the finer points of printing. Soon, as fully trained *journeymen*, they would be ready to accept work in other towns.

Another member of the family was Anna, Lysbeth's attractive eighteen-year-old daughter. At the moment her mother suspected that she was in love with the boy across the street. Lysbeth had noted all the usual signs of a budding romance – the wreath of greenery he had attached to their front door, and later the little posy he had delivered with his card and name. Anna obviously liked him, and had shyly placed another little bunch of flowers on her window sill, complete with a romantic note (copied from a book). Lysbeth knew that if everything went well there would be formal calls from the lad, while she and her husband tactfully left the room, and she expected an engagement by Christmas with the solemn exchange of rings and a coin cut in two. (She still possessed her own half coin Pieter had given her twenty-five years ago, and her father-in-law's gift of a workbox full of needles, thread and scissors.)

The other children, all boys, were still at school. Hendrick attended the secondary school or Latin school. He was studying Latin, Greek and French, and hoped later to go like his brother to Leyden university. The two smaller boys, Adriaen and Dirck were somewhat lazy, much preferring to sail boats, or play marbles and hopscotch than to work hard. They went to Mr Veer's private school down the road (one of many with the name of the teacher on a sign hanging outside the door). They seemed backward in their reading and writing, and ignorant of the Scriptures, in spite of frequent beatings from Mr Veer and their father. Lysbeth wondered whether the time had not come for them to be removed to another private school where the master would be stricter still.

In winter months Lysbeth sat indoors in her warm housecoat (for the peat fire gave out little heat) and toasted her toes in a footwarmer. This was a square metal box, pierced with holes, and containing a slowly burning piece of peat. There were several such boxes, and Pieter had his own footwarmer in the office, too. She passed the time reading the States Bible or her favourite poems by Jacob Cats, knitting or making lace.

About six o'clock Pieter returned from the office, and after

A homely Dutch scene. Notice the warming pan on the wall for use in the box bed (P. de Hooch, Maternal Duty*)*

they had strolled along by the canal, and he had read the latest news in the gazette, they prepared for the guests they had invited to the evening meal at eight. Instead of the usual oil lamps, Lysbeth had lighted tallow candles in their fine brass chandelier; candles were expensive and used on special occasions only. Every kind of pottery dish, pewter bowl and glass covered her fine embroidered table cloth, and there were many dainties. Apart from the usual beer, there was wine spiced with cloves, cinnamon and ginger, and caudle, a white wine sweetened with a stick of cinnamon. Lysbeth had made hutsepot (vegetable and meat stew); there was a variety of crabs, lobster and other shellfish, and some delicious pancakes and fruit. Much of the

Music-making (Jan Steen)

food was eaten with the fingers and a knife, the guests wiping their greasy hands on the damask napkins she had thoughtfully provided.

The meal was followed by a musical entertainment, singing duets, playing the *viol*, flute and harpsichord, and games with cards and dice. By ten o'clock, when the drums of the civic guard sounded in the streets below, the guests collected their lanterns, and began to stroll homeward. Lysbeth and Pieter climbed into their fourposter bed, to discuss the success of the evening, and plan their next party.

4   A Trip to the Country

It was a hot and sunny summer morning in May, and the English visitors had decided that a trip into the neighbouring country-side would make a welcome change from the bustle of Amsterdam. At first there was some discussion whether the outing should be made by road or by water. Should they take the stage coach running regularly between Amsterdam and the towns nearby? It was a long open cart, drawn by four horses, and had huge iron wheels and a covering of coarse canvas. However a journey by coach required an early start, and most of the English party, already experienced travellers in many parts of Europe, knew full well that a journey over bumpy, dusty roads, with deep ruts, would be a hardship rather than a pleasure, even although many of the roads were lined with shady linden trees offering protection from the strong sun.

THE WATER COACH

So it was decided to take the water coach. One of the party had chanced by good fortune to buy a traveller's guide from the leading Amsterdam bookseller. It was a most useful book which gave the times of coach and boat trips, the names of inns (the Pelican at Haarlem was apparently particularly good) and interesting details about local fairs, markets and churches. The party was relieved to know that it was even possible to travel back to Amsterdam quite late at night.

The water coach proved to be a comfortable, long boat, rely-ing on sail and the occasional help of horses which pulled it with ropes along the towpath by the canal. It had a large awning to cover the passengers from sudden rain, and neat, well

scrubbed wooden benches. The decks were spotlessly clean.

The English party eyed with interest the forty or so passengers on board, for the boat was nearly full. People of all kinds were travelling that day, homely peasant women, with large empty baskets and full purses, who had sold their village produce in the Amsterdam market early that morning and were returning home, a *predikant* on his way to a village funeral, one or two quite well-to-do ladies and gentlemen who seemed to mix quite happily with the more simple folk. In a corner seat sat a merchant studying his account books, and a group of children, who had been fairly quiet while they consumed a substantial breakfast of bread and cheese, now started a sing-song, and blew on penny whistles. The bargeman seemed to be expecting this, and handed out songbooks with music, and soon nearly everyone was joining in the local folk songs.

William Temple was much impressed by the flatness of Holland, the large number of canals and boats and how these helped the Dutch to travel easily and transport their goods cheaply. Men lost no time, as they could eat, write and sleep while they travelled. Everywhere there was a forest of sails, and canals linked every village and farmhouse.

The journey by boat was smooth and leisurely, an ideal way of seeing the surrounding countryside. From time to time they stopped at a village, and a little bell rang to let travellers know that the boat was about to depart again. They glided past patches of marshland and willow trees, and solitary fishermen with their rods catching bream and perch. Suddenly there would be a flurry of wings among the rushes, and wild duck whirred into the air. They could see for miles across the flat Dutch country-side, the skyline broken by a windmill, or church spire and a network of canals and *dykes*.

There was plenty to watch: cattle peacefully grazing in the fields (the milkmaids would travel by boat to milk them) or a little wooden bridge raised as they passed by, a cluster of villagers waiting by the roadside, and waving as they went through. The

Dutch countryside and windmill (J. van Ruisdael, Mill at Wijk*)*

road ran for much of the way alongside the canal on a raised causeway bounded by stately poplars, and along it could be seen horsemen riding, or the stage coaches with their hooded covers rumbling by. Occasionally the coaches stopped at a toll gate with a little box nailed by the side. The coachman alighted and put the necessary money inside and the coach passed on. Apparently, the English visitors were told, the box was emptied by the tollkeeper every few days when he had time.

THE COUNTRY PEASANTS

By the canal side there were pleasant country houses, some of them used by wealthy Amsterdam businessmen for country holidays. They had neat tiled roofs and brightly painted shutters.

A country house of a well-to-do family (P. de Hooch, A Country Cottage*)*

In their brick paved courtyards, sheltered by trailing greenery, their well-to-do owners and friends could be seen, sitting at little tables, drinking beer, smoking and playing cards. There were also the tumbledown cottages of the less prosperous peasants. These had thatched roofs, and walls of mud and wood. Smoke came from a hole in the roof, and their miserable windows had a sort of reed latticework instead of glass or shutters, and let in little light. In the doorway some rather grubby children could be seen playing with marbles and a top amongst a clutter of wooden barrels and old earthenware pots. The family *clogs* were scattered outside the front door ready for when they were needed for a journey along the muddy cart track to the well or cowshed. The father of the household could shape a new pair in an afternoon, skilfully scooping out a round hollow for the feet from the soft wood, and carefully shaping round the heel.

Temple decided that the boors, or country peasants, were rather slow witted but honest people. They fed mostly on herbs, roots and milk and had a hard life, but seemed contented with their lot.

COUNTRY FESTIVITIES

It was now midday, and time to stop at one of the many pleasant inns which bordered the canal. The English visitors had heard encouraging stories of how good the food and drink could be, and they were not disappointed. Freshly caught fish, accompanied by wholemeal bread and butter and ripe cheese, were served by the innkeeper. Then followed delightful pancakes and a delicious kind of junket of lemon and sour cream. Some of the party experimented with the national dish – a kind of stew called hutsepot. It was made of chopped meat and vegetables such as turnips, onions and parsnips, spiced with ginger, and was pronounced very tasty. Everyone seemed to be drinking large quantities of beer and wine, for the Dutch had a reputation for being fond of their food and drink.

Opposite *Musicians at a cottage door (Adriaen van Ostade)*

The party had scarcely finished eating their lunch, when they heard the sounds of noise and laughter outside, and were told that a village wedding party was approaching. A gaily decorated farm cart containing the bride and groom rumbled up, soon followed by a throng of wedding guests.

By looking through a little window into the courtyard of the inn, the English visitors could observe undetected the whole proceedings (though it is doubtful whether any of the wedding party would have noticed them anyway). The little courtyard had been festooned with flowers and trailing greenery, and two chairs decorated with hanging fabrics in honour of the bride and groom, who were dressed in their best clothes. The bride's dress was black (so it could be used for family mournings later) but on this occasion it was lightened by attractive ribbons and gay flowers.

The young couple were offered a cup of brandy, and the groom a gaily decorated tobacco pipe, and, amid much merriment, the party sat down at a table splendidly filled with plates of food of every kind and innumerable tankards of drink. From time to time there would be a lull, and some of the guests drew little scrolls of parchment from a wicker basket, and read out verses composed in honour of the lucky pair. When all had eaten and drunk their fill, a musical trio started to play on bag-pipes and flutes. The festivities would end in a whirl of dancing, but this would continue late into the evening, and long before this our English visitors were back again in the water coach.

They aimed to reach Haarlem shortly, in time to enjoy the local *kermis*, a festival held in many of the villages and towns of Holland, and an occasion they had been told they must not miss. The kermis in Haarlem, one of the biggest, and organised by the town authorities, was already well under way, having been opened early in the month with a resounding peal of bells from the town hall. It was the second week, and nearing the end of the festivities, yet the town was still thronged with people, and everyone was obviously in holiday mood.

Opposite *Peasants merrymaking (Jan Steen,* A Village Fair*)*

Peasants at a kermis. The quack doctor and his assistants are extracting a tooth (Jan Steen, The Quack*)*

Booths and stalls with gaily decorated awnings had been erected in the market square, and all the open spaces near the town centre. People from Haarlem, and the neighbouring villages for miles around, crowded into the area. An especially brisk trade was being done in attractively shaped kermis cakes covered with loving messages in sugar icing which the young men were busy buying for their sweethearts. There were stalls to cater for all tastes, selling ribbons, jewellery, flowers, clay pipes with long stems, attractive pottery, ballads, music sheets and instruments. Bagpipes, fiddles, whistles, and drums played cheerful tunes; there were puppet shows, clowns, performing dogs, dwarfs, fire eaters, tame bears, tightrope walkers, and all the fun of the fair. Especially happy were the children, buying sweets, and paper windmills on sticks, wooden dolls, marbles and painted hoops and tops. It would be a long time to wait till another kermis next May. They envied grandmother who told tales of the days she remembered when there was a kermis in September as well as in May, and she had seen the one-eyed sailor from the distant east with a weird sea creature in a green glass bottle.

5 The Artist's Studio

During a stay, however short, in Holland, most foreigners noticed the extraordinary number of paintings on sale everywhere. Even quite humble homes had several 'original' pictures on the walls, and they could be seen in shops, orphanages and even forges. The English visitor John Evelyn noticed at the great annual fair at Rotterdam that ordinary farmers were spending hundreds of pounds on pictures. In no other country in Europe did the man in the street take such an interest in art.

William Temple also may have bought some Dutch pictures while he was in Holland though he says nothing about Dutch art in his 'Observations'. A few years before he had had his own portrait painted in England by a Dutch artist Peter Lely who had settled there. Some of Temple's party are likely to have visited an artist's studio, for groups of artists were working in all the chief towns of Holland – Leyden, Delft, and Haarlem, as well as Amsterdam.

THE ARTIST AT WORK

Imagine a visit to such a studio, the well-lighted room of a middle or working class Dutch home. Inside would be a clutter of easels, canvas, palettes, draperies, stools and other 'props', and the heavy smell of oil paints and turpentine. Several apprentices, aged from eleven to seventeen, would be busy at work under their master's eye, for, having completed a brief schooling in the three R's, they would start on a long and hard training. During their apprenticeship with the artist they would sleep with his children in the attic, eat meals prepared by his wife, and be soundly beaten by the master if they failed to mix their paints

A Dutch artist busy in his studio (Vermeer, Die Allegorie der Malerei*)*

properly, or spoilt a canvas by skimping their work. There was nothing speedy or slovenly about Dutch art; the artists had practised for years, and studied in detail, the folds of drapery, the glitter of light on glass or the bloom on the skin of a peach.

Fathers, too, trained their sons, and often several members of one family became gifted painters.

The artist himself had paid his fees to the artists' guild of Saint Luke, a kind of trade union to which he had to belong, and whose rules he must obey. If he moved to another town he had to be elected to the guild of his new town. Most artists were glad of the help given by the guild; sometimes it might sell some of their paintings at an *auction* attended by important people in the town, after which everyone would enjoy some beer and spiced cakes as refreshment. When the artist was in real trouble the guild might provide food and clothing for his family, and help him in his extreme poverty or old age. For in spite of the great demand for paintings, these were cheap, and the artists were rather looked down upon by other people. After a lifetime of producing beautiful paintings, many of them died in great poverty and neglect. The family of Frans Hals ended their days in the poor house at Haarlem, and Rembrandt went bankrupt. Vermeer had to pawn his pictures to buy bread, and Jan Steen was glad to work as an innkeeper because he could not afford to live on his earnings as a painter: he left five hundred unsold pictures at his death.

TYPES OF DUTCH PAINTINGS

Any artist who hopes to sell his pictures rather than merely paint for his own delight has to please the people who will buy his work. He must appeal to their taste and interests, even if these are not the same as his own. All this had a great effect on seventeenth-century Dutch painting.

In the Middle Ages the great *patron* of artists was the Church, and sculptors, painters and craftsmen of all kinds were busily employed building cathedrals and churches, and decorating them with beautiful stained glass, altar pieces, and religious paintings. But the Dutch had broken away from the Catholic Church in the sixteenth century, and set up simple Protestant churches of their own. These had plain whitewashed walls inside, and few religious pictures, which were frowned upon as being too 'Catholic'. A few Dutch people bought religious paintings of the birth of Christ or the Crucifixion, but, in general, there was not a great demand for these. The Dutch found inspiration for their faith by reading their Bible at home, or by listening attentively to the long sermons in church rather than gazing at religious paintings.

In most other European countries, especially England, Spain and France, it was not the common people but the king and nobles for whom the artists catered. These wanted formal, flattering portraits showing the upper classes in their elegant silk and velvet clothes. They were not interested in scenery unless they themselves figured prominently in the foreground, and they would certainly not have wished to hang on the walls of their splendid mansions any homely pictures of such things as country weddings, uproar in the village school, or red lobsters and bunches of onions.

Holland had no king, and the nobles were few and rather unimportant. The people who mattered, and who had money, were the wealthy merchants and traders, the respectable citizens of the towns who sat on the town council, ran the local orphanage and hospital, and organised the home guard of soldiers who defended the town. Some of them liked to be painted in their Sunday best, so they welcomed a good artist to depict the shimmer of silk, the fluffy warmth of fur on dresses, and fine velvet cloaks. If they were gifted and musical, it was pleasant to have their family and friends painted at a musical evening, performing on viols, *lute* and harpsichord, or playing cards. In the background might be well draped tables, laden with silver, goblets, shining glass, and attractive bowls of *luscious* fruit. But many were content to have homely portraits of themselves, and scenes of the town in which they lived or the countryside nearby. Above all, the pictures must be small, so as to fit easily into the small rooms of a town house, and very detailed and interesting, so that their owners could study them at home during the long, dull winter hours.

Occasionally, of course, officials might require other larger works, decorations on the walls of schools, *almshouses* or the town hall (the new one at Amsterdam, begun in 1648, provided

39

plenty of chance for painting). Some might require group portraits of officers or committees which would in our day be shown by a photograph rather than a painting. Dutch artists learned to specialise, so that they became experts, and spent their whole lives doing one kind of painting.

STILL LIFE AND LANDSCAPES

Some painters catered largely for the lower classes (though the upper classes, too, bought their work) and did scenes of 'low life' which would hardly have been accepted as art in other countries. These showed homely drinking scenes in taverns, skating and sliding on the ice, peasant girls selling food, fishermen at their nets, and children playing every conceivable game. The characters might sometimes be old, untidy and dirty, but they were true to life, and showed the people as the artist knew

Opposite *A Dutch family group (Frans Hals)*

Below *The fishmarket at Leyden. The houses have steep gabled roofs (Jan Steen)*

them. Jan Steen was one of these realistic, homely artists. You will find some of his pictures in this book. He sometimes even tried hopefully to improve his fellow countrymen by pointing out their weaknesses, as in one of his pictures called 'The Effects of Drunkenness'. The whole household is shown in confusion, books and furniture scattered on the floor. While the drunken father and mother lie asleep, the baby ruins the violin bow, other children steal from the mother, the cat paws at the bird-cage, and the dog has jumped on the crumpled tablecloth and is devouring the family dinner.

The Dutch had a great love of the countryside, and were among the first people in Europe to paint landscape. Flat scenery is often thought uninteresting by people used to hills and mountains, but it has often inspired some of the best art both in Holland and in England. One of the attractions of a flat countryside is the wide expanse of sky; sunsets, sunrise and cloud effects can be very beautiful. Some Dutch artists spent their whole lives painting not portraits but scenery. Often only the bottom third of the picture shows the land, for much of the interest lies in the top two-thirds showing sky: blue sky with fleecy clouds, stormy, glowering sky, or the pale delicate sky seen through an early morning mist or hazy rain. In the fore-ground placid cows may graze on rich grass, in the background are trees, and the distant church spire and a windmill break the far skyline. The whole scene radiates peace, and it is easy to forget that Holland was often at war in the seventeenth cen-tury, but then the Dutch were not very interested in painting scenes of war.

The winter scenes are very attractive too. The dark silhouettes of trees and simple peasant homes stand out against the snow, and frozen rivers and canals are full of lively, moving figures, warmly clad in fur hats and colourful cloaks, skating, sliding, playing ice hockey, drawing sledges, roasting oxen over bon-fires, and keeping up their spirits by drinking tankards of spiced ale.

Opposite *A Dutch still-life painting (Floris van Dijck)*

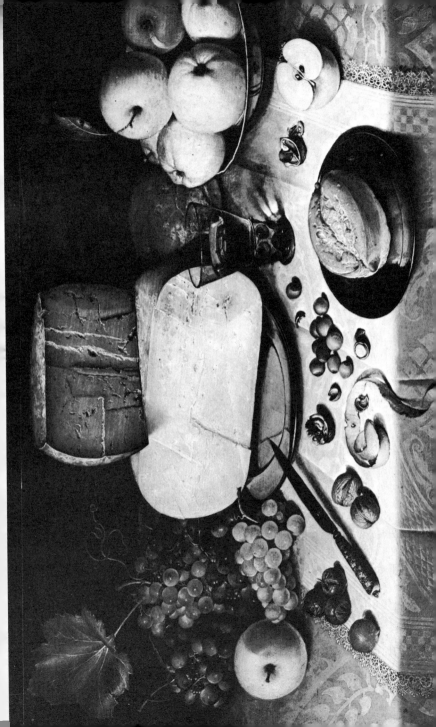

Another kind of art which the Dutch developed in the seventeenth century was *still life*. These paintings were delightful settings of homely objects, often arranged on a white tablecloth: an orange or two, grapes, nuts, a glass full of splendid red wine, crusty loaves of bread and tasty cheeses. The detail is tremendous – peel from the fruit slipping off the knife, reflections in a shining silver dish, or a fly crawling over the oysters. At times there is a riot of colour, or the artist may deliberately concentrate on delicate browns and greys. Occasionally the subjects are a bit too crude for modern taste. Not everyone would appreciate having a picture on the wall of crabs, lobsters, silvery herrings, dead pheasants and joints of uncooked, red meat! But the Dutch relished good food, and such paintings show their delight in the worth of homely things. Smoking had been developed in Europe, with the introduction of tobacco from the New World in the previous century, and this was another of the Dutch pleasures. It is not surprising that many of the still life paintings have, by the pewter tankard of ale, a long-stemmed clay pipe, and sometimes a packet of tobacco as well, complete with carefully written label on the cover.

The Dutch were great gardeners, too, and every well-to-do person hoped to acquire some of the new plants which had been brought back by Dutch travellers overseas. Soon the habit of planting attractive, formal Dutch gardens was spread to other lands by visitors to Holland. William Temple continued to be an enthusiastic gardener while in the Netherlands, and on his return to England planted a Dutch garden. One flower that became a craze was the tulip, introduced into Holland from Constantinople at the end of the sixteenth century. It was grown commercially in the sandy area around Haarlem (Holland still remains the leading bulb-growing country in the world) and all kinds of experiments were made to produce tulips of different colours and sizes. People paid fantastic sums to acquire rare bulbs, and fortunes were often made if the bulbs grew successfully, or lost if they failed. Many tulips are to be found in Dutch paintings, but there are also colourful arrangements of flowers of all kinds, beautifully painted down to the fallen petal or the tiny drops of dew on a leaf.

You can work out from these paintings how many of our garden flowers were known to people in the seventeenth century. There are sunflowers, irises, bluebells, guelder roses and many others. In the best manner of floral arrangement they did not mind mixing wild grasses and wild flowers like buttercups and daisies with their garden flowers, and their paintings are full of these too. Another surprising thing is the great amount of 'life' lurking in these 'still' paintings. Often you can count up to ten different varieties: moths, ladybirds, spiders, butterflies, all accurately and faithfully painted in their minuteness.

PAINTERS OF SHIPS

Boats, too, played a large part in Dutch people's lives, and there are paintings of boats of all kinds: huge East Indiamen sailing to the colonies, herring *busses* and whalers, barges laden with cheeses and timber on the canals, delicate, gaily decorated yachts in the harbour, carrying foreign royalty on their state visits to Holland.

Rather special artists of *seascapes* were William Van de Velde, and his son, also called William. The father Van de Velde had been a sailor since he was a boy, and before he was twenty his careful drawings of ships of all kinds came to the notice of the Dutch government. They decided to make him an official war artist, a very unusual appointment in those days. He went with the navy on all kinds of voyages, and was required to do accurate drawings of battle scenes where there was plenty of action. He had a very exciting time with Admiral Tromp when he was sweeping the English off the seas in the 1650s, and was in the thick of many battles against the English and the Swedes.

Later in his life William Van de Velde and his son came to England. By this time the wars with England were over, and Charles II who, during his exile in Holland, had met the father and admired him, asked them both to paint scenes of English ships and sea battles. The family settled in very happily at Greenwich (the centre of the Admiralty), were given generous

45

salaries by the king, and produced hundreds of drawings and paintings of ships – rough pencil sketches, delicate Indian ink drawings and finished canvases in oils. Many of them can still be seen in the National Gallery, London, at Hampton Court, or in the National Maritime Museum at Greenwich. When a Dutchman became king of England as William III, they probably felt even more at home. They spent the rest of their lives in England, and were buried in a churchyard in London.

6 Rembrandt in Amsterdam and Frans Hals in Haarlem

Rembrandt was an old man, nearing the end of his life when Sir William Temple came to Holland. He was highly respected as one of the greatest painters of the age, yet at this time he was living modestly and somewhat neglected in humble lodgings in one of the poorer districts of Amsterdam. When he died in the autumn of 1669 he was buried quietly in the Wester Kerk, and his death went largely unnoticed in the outside world.

REMBRANDT'S EARLY LIFE

Rembrandt's great gift for painting had been revealed at quite an early age. His family were prosperous millers owning mills in Leyden, a fine city second only in size to Amsterdam. They had high hopes that he might become a scholar. He did briefly attend Leyden university, but his urge to paint became strong and his family soon knew that he must be a painter. He had already started using his brothers and sisters as models and he did many portraits of his mother. The later ones show a determined old lady full of character, and are among his finest. She was obviously a strong influence on his life.

Like all Dutch artists Rembrandt had a careful apprenticeship in the art of painting, working part of the time in his home town Leyden, and also in Amsterdam. After 1632 he lived permanently in this great city, seldom travelling far outside it, and never abroad. When asked once why he did not visit Italy, the great centre of art, he replied that he was far too busy. For him Amsterdam was the hub of the world, providing every kind of subject an artist could desire, a city of bustling activity, but one where he could work undisturbed. A Frenchman,

Rembrandt's patron Constantyn Huygens (de Keyser)

Descartes, said of Amsterdam: 'Everyone is so occupied in furthering their own interests that I could spend the whole of my life there without being noticed by a soul.'

The artist was often helped by a noble patron, and Rembrandt was fortunate as a young man in coming to the notice of a brilliant courtier called Constantyn Huygens. Huygens had travelled widely in Italy and England, where he was knighted by the English king, and had great love for English poetry some of which he translated into Dutch. He held an important post as Secretary to Frederick Henry, Prince of Orange, whose family was the most powerful in the Netherlands. Huygens must have been one of the most *versatile* men of his day. He spoke several languages well, studied *astronomy*, law and the Scriptures, was a keen musician, and a great lover of art. As a young man he was very athletic too, once even climbing to the top of the spire of Strasbourg cathedral. He persuaded the Prince of Orange to let Rembrandt paint a number of religious paintings for him. This, of course, meant that other people also wanted to buy his pictures.

Rembrandt's fame in Amsterdam at this time was spread by a very unusual painting called 'The Anatomy Lesson of Professor Tulp'. People knew little about surgery in those days, and seventeenth-century doctors would have been amazed to learn of twentieth-century miracles, such as heart and liver transplants, and artificial lungs. It was not easy to learn about the human body because of the difficulty of obtaining dead bodies for doctors to examine. People had not become used to the idea of helping to further medical knowledge by giving their bodies for use in research when they died, and the Church thought *dissection* was wrong. Very occasionally, however, the body of a dead criminal could be used, and the doctors would carefully examine tissues, muscles and organs. Sometimes interested members of the public attended, too, and Rembrandt was one of these. He painted a picture of what was probably the only dissection in Amsterdam in 1632, an important occasion.

49

Professor Tulp gives an anatomy lesson (Rembrandt)

Professor Tulp was one of the most famous doctors of his day, and a man of many interests, and considerable wealth. He had helped to run the local university, was city treasurer, a magistrate, and had many artistic friends. In the painting Rembrandt shows the doctors and spectators crowding round, watching intently, as Tulp explains a point about the arm muscles. The corpse from Leyden (Rembrandt's home town) was that of a criminal who had been hanged for committing a violent robbery. Notice how different the scene is from that in a modern operating theatre: no masks, white overalls, or helpful nurses. The figures are dressed in their everyday clothes, with large clean white collars, and Tulp, as it is a formal occasion, wears a hat. (This was quite usual during church services, attending parliament at The Hague or even while visiting friends' homes.)

Through Professor Tulp Rembrandt was probably introduced to a number of interesting people, and he painted many portraits of doctors, writers, publishers, and prosperous business men. He had several Jewish friends as sitters (Jews were flourishing in Holland, although not so well treated in many other European countries at this time). He painted or made *etchings* of many different subjects – religious themes, Amsterdam beggars, eastern foreigners and Negroes, even lions and elephants from a travelling circus.

Rembrandt wrote no detailed diary, and the business records about him are very scanty. However, every few years he looked into the mirror and did a self-portrait. These provide a fascinating glimpse of the painter. The early ones show him as a rather awkward, determined young man, with strong eyes and a large *bulbous* nose. He might put on a gay velvet hat and a dashing cloak on such an occasion to look like a prince, or don a few rags and imagine himself as a beggar. Often he was in dusty working clothes, and could not bear to be interrupted. A frank critic wrote: 'The ugly and *plebeian* face by which he was illfavoured was accompanied by untidy and dirty clothes, since it was his custom when working to wipe his brushes on himself.' Later portraits show him as the successful painter (sometimes

A self portrait by Rembrandt

with brush in hand), but there is a wistful sadness about some of the very late ones, for Rembrandt had a hard life.

One of the liveliest of Rembrandt's pictures is one he painted of himself with his new bride Saskia. She came of a well-connected family, and Rembrandt had obviously made a good match. They were extremely happy together. Rembrandt paints himself with a roguish grin on his face, and a fashionable hat with a white feather on his head. Saskia, in a fine green frock, sits on his lap, as he waves a glass of wine gaily in the air. It was probably one of the happiest moments in Rembrandt's life.

In 1639 they moved into an attractive house in a more fashionable part of Amsterdam. It had an imposing front door and fine windows. It still stands in the city, largely unchanged, although the roof was altered after Rembrandt's time. The price was really more than the artist could afford, and from then on most of his life was to be dogged by heavy debts. Some of Saskia's family complained that the young couple were living extravagantly, and beyond their means. Rembrandt liked to attend sales, and buy up etchings and work by other artists. He said he was prepared to pay high prices 'in order to *enhance* the *prestige* of his profession'. He was training apprentices, which brought in some fees, and selling pictures to important sitters. It was as well that the new house was a large one, for he had a large collection of drawings and works of art, and a great deal of 'clutter' in his studio – swords, armour, draperies etc. which provided useful backgrounds for his sitters.

This was, nevertheless, a sad time, for three of their children had died as babies a few weeks old, and it was no consolation to remember that this often happened at the time in which they lived. However, the fourth child survived, a lusty young son called Titus who became a great joy to his father. Rembrandt did many portraits of the boy, often shown at a table sketching, for Titus was artistic, but, of course, could not match his father's brilliance.

A few months after Titus was born, Saskia died, and was buried at the Oude Kerk at Amsterdam. She was probably never very strong, and she and Rembrandt had been married only eight years. He must have felt very lonely and sad after Saskia's 53

death, and wandered on the outskirts of Amsterdam, doing rough drawings of the countryside around the city, brilliant impressions of the river, windmills, and bridges. About this time he finished what has been considered by many people his masterpiece – the famous 'Night Watch'. It shows officers of the town guard of Amsterdam, with their swords, pikes and drums, a fine group of figures *silhouetted* against a dark background.

He now needed someone to look after Titus and manage his household, for, like many artistic people, Rembrandt did not like doing housework. After a very unsatisfactory nurse had been dismissed, he found the perfect answer in Hendrickje Stoffels. She was a cheerful and practical person who became devoted to Rembrandt and to Titus. She was a model for some of Rembrandt's pictures, cooked and cleaned the house, brought up Titus, and later, when Rembrandt had got into dreadful financial muddles, helped Titus to sort out the debts. There is a story that one day Rembrandt painted a lifelike portrait of Hendrickje and propped it up at the window of his house. It was so realistic that it was some time before neighbours realised that it was not a real person.

Towards the end of his life Rembrandt became a rather lonely figure. His pupils, once trained, moved away to work in other towns, and he had few close friends among his fellow artists. Influential and important people came more rarely to his studio for portraits, and he was piling up more and heavier debts. In the 1650s many Dutch people were very hard hit financially by the war with England, and Rembrandt was one of them. He had spent too lavishly buying other artists' work for his collections, and he still owed half the money for his fine house. Soon he had the bitter experience of seeing all his best furniture, clothes, *porcelain* and glass up for auction, and his etchings and seventy of his best paintings fetching low prices in the salerooms. (Others were hard hit, too, and it was not a good time for selling.) He was forced to move from his fine house into humbler lodgings. Towards the end of his life he

Opposite *Rembrandt's house in Amsterdam*

continued to produce fine paintings, but he was becoming more sad and lonely. Hendrickje died, and some time later, his beloved son Titus. Within a year Rembrandt, too, was buried beside him in the great Wester Kerk in Amsterdam.

FRANS HALS

While Rembrandt was producing his masterpieces at Amsterdam, the great painter Frans Hals was busily painting magnificent portraits in the little neighbouring town of Haarlem. This was a flourishing place in the seventeenth century, with attractive red brick gabled houses and a busy market, dominated by the majestic cathedral of St Bavo. Brewing and *textiles* were its main industries, and bulb-growing was beginning in the surrounding countryside. Haarlem had many gifted artists. Opposite is a picture by one of them. It shows the fine town hall and gabled shops with signs hanging outside the doors. Businessmen of the town are gossiping in the spacious market-place, spotlessly clean as in many Dutch towns, and in the distance the tower of St Bavo's can be glimpsed.

The Hals family were obviously artistic (two of Hals's brothers were painters too) and more than any other painter he brought to life the people of seventeenth-century Holland. Hals did not bother about rough drawings, but painted boldly and directly on the canvas. He did hundreds of portraits, but each is an individual character, arresting as a modern photograph. There is usually a light, plain background, uncluttered by draperies and fussy furniture. The only sign of the sitter's rank is perhaps a little *coat of arms* hanging on a nail above his head.

Here can be seen the worthy citizens of Haarlem in their Sunday best for the occasion, the men wearing hats and sporting neat little clipped moustaches and small pointed beards. The women wear dark, rustling dresses, and their hair is almost entirely covered with a variety of delightful muslin caps. The lace on collars and cuffs is done with a delicate touch – some collars stand stiffly round the wearer's neck like a pie frill, others droop softly down over the shoulders in neat folds. The sitters

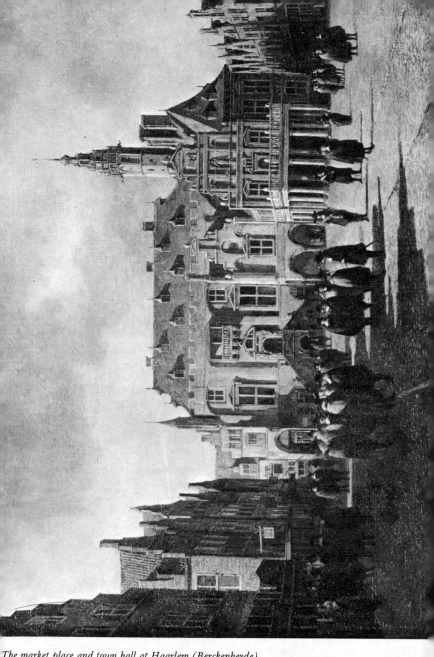

The market place and town hall at Haarlem (Berckenheyde)

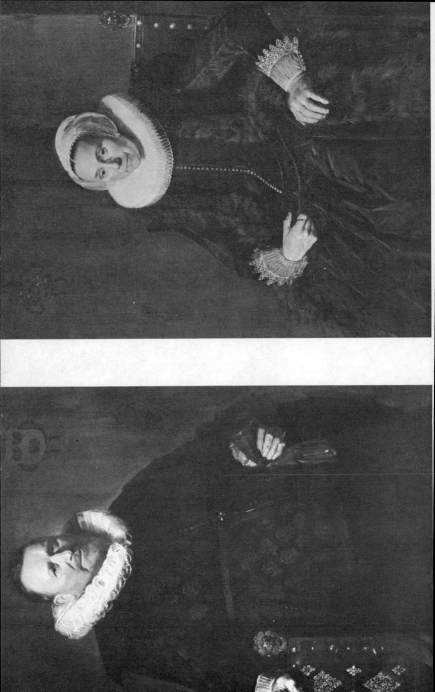

obviously paid great attention to fashions in such matters. Hals has made the hands wonderfully expressive, portraying them realistically in a variety of positions; the ladies' fingers *decorously* holding a fan, locket or cherished Bible, the gentlemen clasping gloves or a hat. Another seventeenth-century artist, Van Dyck, is reputed to have said of Hals, 'I have never known anyone who has such a power over his brush'.

A TIME OF TROUBLES

All his life Frans Hals had a desperate struggle against grinding poverty. He had a large family to maintain (two children by his first wife Anna, and ten children, although some of them died young, by his second wife Lysbeth). The latter was a poor simple woman who could not even write her name. She signed papers, as *illiterates* did in those days, by making a cross, but she worked hard to help her family. They had many sorrows; one son, called Pieter, an *imbecile*, had to be brought up in the Haarlem workhouse, and his clothes and food provided by city funds. Lysbeth later had the shame of going to the mayor to say that they could not support their eldest daughter Sara and her baby in the Hals household, and she, too, had to go into the workhouse. Frequently the family was too poor to buy bread and shoes for the children, but the artists' guild allowed Hals to remain a member, although he could not always afford to pay his subscription.

It is tragic to think that a great painter like Hals could not support himself by his work, but at least in seventeenth-century Holland more was done for the poor than in many other countries. Haarlem had its workhouse, orphanage, hospital, and old people's homes, and the city authorities generously lent the painter money, and provided fuel during the cold winter months. In gratitude for their kindness Hals painted a superb group portrait of the Governors of St Elizabeth Hospital. Four of the governors are listening attentively to a suggestion being made by the man in the foreground. Notice their sombre clothes and hats, worn at a formal business meeting. The table has books, an inkwell, and pens lying on a dark 59

Above: The governors of Haarlem hospital (Frans Hals). Below: The committee of ladies who ran the old people's home in Haarlem (Frans Hals)

green tablecloth. The map on the wall shows the Dutch interest in travel overseas. Hals has made all his figures individual characters – their faces reveal their personalities.

In another group portrait Hals painted, the ladies who governed the old people's home are soberly dressed in dark grey gowns, and have pleasant homely faces. You feel they would be kind to those in real need, but firm in their attitude to lazy scroungers. The old lady second from the left, called Marijtje Willems, was seventy-three when Hals painted this picture, but still a very active person. We know from the Haarlem records that two years earlier she had been visiting the Hals household when his daughter Sara's baby was born, and she was one of the committee that agreed to admit Sara to the workhouse.

The city of Haarlem's last assistance to Frans Hals is shown in the entry for September 1666. Four florins were paid into the gravemakers' accounts for 'an opening [grave] in the cathedral for Mr Frans Hals'. During all his difficulties he had never lost hope, or his faith in human beings, and, in spite of all his troubles, most of his portraits show lively, good-humoured faces. Appropriately, Frans Hals is best remembered by his portrait 'The Laughing Cavalier'.

7 The Dutch Settlers Overseas

Few Europeans had visited the East in the Middle Ages, but legends of its fabulous wealth had long inspired explorers, and at the end of the fifteenth century a few adventurous Portuguese pushed round the Cape of Good Hope to India, and to Malacca in Malaya.

On the summit of Malacca's grassy hill stood a palace from which Malay sultans ruled a huge empire in the East. In the rivers lay junks from China and India, canoes from Malay rivers, and sailing boats of all kinds from islands far to the south and east. Malacca was the greatest port of the East, and in its crowded streets could be found traders in luxuries of all sorts, Chinese porcelain, jewels, silver, jade and spices. By 1511 the Portuguese had successfully captured the flourishing port, and from the fortress nearby soon dominated the trade of all this part of the East. Their huge *carracks*, laden with jewels; spices and silks, sailed back to Lisbon, making Portugal one of the richest countries in Europe, and arousing the jealousy of English and Dutch merchants who longed to make their fortunes too. Their chance came in the seventeenth century when Portugal, now ruled by Spain, became weaker, and her ships fell an easy prey to English and Dutch rivals. By 1640 Malacca, though but a shadow of its former glory, fell to the Dutch, and everywhere the islands, too, came under their influence.

Nowhere was the lure of the East felt more than in Amsterdam with its wharves full of ships and barges, and inns where old seadogs recounted stirring tales of their adventures at sea. 63

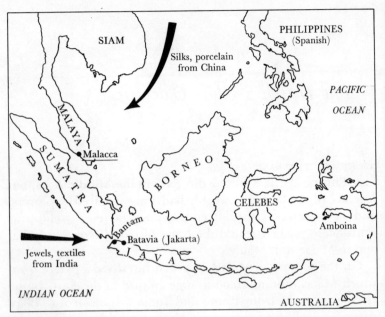

Spice Islands or East Indies

English and Dutch ships attacking a Portuguese carrack in the East. Notice the flags, and the heavy guns

Here were skilled shipwrights, *cordwainers* and carpenters; here one could buy the best world globes in Europe, and charts, especially Lucas Wagenaer's wonderful maps showing buoys, anchorages and all the aids to safe sailing. With Wagenaer's charts surely anyone could sail to sea with confidence. English rivals of the Dutch were even glad to 'borrow' his charts, affectionately known as Waggoners, and use them, in English translation of course.

And if your *navigation* was shaky, there was no excuse for not improving it. Scores of expert seamen were prepared to tell you all the tricks of the trade, and competed with each other to attract business by nailing on the doors of their house pieces of paper with mathematical problems, and their solutions, to intrigue the passerby and arouse his admiration in their navigational skill.

THE DUTCH EAST INDIA COMPANY

There were always plenty of sailors in Amsterdam, and other ports of Holland, for the lure of the sea, in spite of its dangers, was strong. These men were keen to travel (although the pay was low, fifteen guilders a month, and only ten on the dangerous voyage to the Spice Islands). Most of the crew had volunteered, whereas in England officials, forming a *press gang*, went round the ports and 'pressed' or forced likely young men to go to sea. In Holland many sailors were always found hanging round the ports for work. It was exciting, too, to visit the shipyards. Special pride was taken in constructing the East Indiamen, as the merchant ships to the East were called, and the building yards at Zaandam near Amsterdam were usually busy. Building the huge vessels employed hundreds of carpenters, craftsmen and painters, who could be seen tarring, *caulking* below the waterline, or painting elaborate decorations on the high ornamental sterns.

These powerful ships were owned by the Dutch East India Company, founded in 1602, which had the sole right to trade in the lands beyond the Cape of Good Hope. Thousands of people invested their hard-earned money in this company

Nauw Mercator riæ Hollandicæ Societis In dæ Orientalis

Caulking East Indiamen. The coat of arms of Amsterdam is shown on the stern

which often made high profits of 20–50 per cent. Most important were the seventeen Directors who ran it. They had been given by the Dutch parliament not only control of the trade, but permission to make treaties with local rulers, wage wars, and build forts and defences. In fact the seventeen Directors were much more interested in trade than conquest and few of them had ever visited the East. They preferred to live a gracious life in Holland, and their beautiful houses overlooking the canals in the fashionable quarter of Amsterdam, were among the finest in the whole country.

THE VOYAGE

The fleets sailed to the East in September, December and April. The voyage took six or seven months, so the ships were large enough to carry the provisions and cargo required for a long period. There were also dangers from pirates, and sailors of enemy countries, anxious to seize a rich prize, so they carried heavy guns and were armed like warships. Being heavy ships they needed more and complicated sails, and therefore more sailors. The Dutch East Indiamen had three large masts with huge sails, and a square sprit sail to the fore to keep the head of the ship before the wind.

Imagine the discomforts of life at sea on such a long voyage – the cramped quarters below deck as the men lay in their swinging hammocks, the dark ill-*ventilated* ships with hatches and gunports closed in wet and stormy weather, and the greasy smells and smoke arising from the cooking galley. Food was dreary and monotonous – salted meat, thick pea and lentil soup, and dry biscuits which easily went bad in the tropical heat on a long voyage. The drinking water stored in barrels became especially 'stinking', and fleas, rats and cockroaches abounded.

Many men fell sick from *scurvy* caused by a *defective* diet; typhus, pneumonia and disease of all kinds spread rapidly, for there was seldom room to separate the sick sailors from the healthy ones. They complained that their clothes were inadequate, because, although the fleets were sailing to tropical   67 waters, there were often cold periods before they reached their destination. However they accepted savage punishments as part of sea life in those days – 100 lashes, nailing an offender's hand to the mast, and confinement for weeks in iron chains. Many had signed on for five years' service (and the cabin boys for ten) and were kept hopeful by the prospect of a few days' call at some delightful island, like St Helena or Mauritius, where the water barrels could be filled, and they could recover from their seasickness, and eat fresh fruit and vegetables.

On the return trip, when the ship was laden with spices, Chinese silks and porcelain, they could dream of spending their hard earned money in the inns of Amsterdam, drinking and telling stories and selling at a high price the pepper and cloves they had smuggled (contrary to the regulations) back to port in their old wooden seachests.

CONDITIONS IN THE EAST

Were it not for the profits to be had – and the ordinary seamen scarcely shared in these – life in the Spice Islands might well have become unbearable. How different from the pleasant flat landscape of Holland with its placid cows, lush pastures, wide expanse of sky with scudding cloud, and broad horizon, interrupted only by the silhouette of a distant windmill or church spire! How homesick must the settlers have been!

The sudden downpours of torrential rain every day, and the hot, damp climate made everything, then as now, grow fast and *luxuriantly*, and jungle covered the greater part of the islands. Giant trees and ferns, creepers and undergrowth twisted in fantastic patterns, and the dark forests hummed with the buzz of countless insects. Monkeys chattered high in the trees, and swung from creeper to creeper, brilliant butterflies and birds streaked by with a flash of colour. Crocodiles lurked in the muddy rivers, and snakes and lizards in the undergrowth. Here were strange animals – the orang outang, a great, coarse, red-haired ape, over five feet tall, living on his platform in the trees, and a great variety of monkeys, rhinoceros, and honey-bears, wild oxen, and wild pig, porcupine, and the shy little mouse deer, no larger than a hare. In the trees were hundreds of huge hanging bees' nests, parrots, hornbills and strange flying creatures – flying foxes, flying squirrels, and even flying lizards. Yet everywhere there was an unutterable loneliness in the jungle, with its few inhabitants. Life was here, but it was unfamiliar to the new European visitor. By the riverside the natives had burnt a clearing in the forest. There were palm-thatched, untidy houses, standing on stilts above the flood waters, and neat plots of ricefields fringed with shady banana trees. Up and down the river, and out at sea plied delicate fishing boats, with their single sail, and in the trading ports around the coasts there was a throng of life – Chinese craftsmen in wood and silver, traders in the bazaars, owners of junks from the East.

Seldom would the Europeans penetrate far inland, since almost the only means of travelling was by the rivers, lined with *mangrove* swamp and palms, the jungle reaching almost to the water's edge. No doubt there were compensations such as the

A fine bench made by Eastern craftsmen for Europeans in the 17th century.

delicious durian fruit, described enthusiastically by one traveller as like 'a rich brown custard, highly flavoured with almonds, but intermingled with wafts of flavour that call to mind cream cheese, onion sauce and brown sherry', but few Europeans ever penetrated the jungle depths enough to enjoy this delicacy fresh from the trees.

No doubt, too, some of the Dutch naturalists who wandered into the interior enjoyed collecting moths and butterflies. The artists among them certainly painted accurately and skilfully the animals and birds they had discovered. To most Dutchmen, however, the attraction of the East lay in the more valuable crops, cinnamon, cloves and pepper, needed in Europe to season meat during the long winter months, and it was upon these that the Dutch fortunes were based.

LIFE IN BATAVIA

Life in the Dutch eastern trading settlements overseas, whether in India, the East Indies or Ceylon, was in many ways the same. The Dutch insisted on the local people trading with them, and if they refused, fought a brief war which the Dutch usually won because they had superior western guns and better ships. They had little desire to conquer large areas inland. This would involve costly wars, and reduce the profits which they would get from peaceful trading. So soon everyone settled down again, and the local people continued to trade, although now with the Dutch and not the Portuguese. In the trading posts they would build, as the Portuguese had done before them, an impressive fort or castle to defend the town, and also surround it with a strong wooden stockade. The richer merchants would build warehouses, a church, and fine houses, often in the style of those at home. There would be a cluster of poor dwellings nearby for the natives and local traders.

Batavia in Java was one of the most prosperous of the trading bases. Here the Dutch had dug canals, and laid out tree-lined

Opposite *Bantam, a Dutch trading settlement in the East Indies. A strong stockade protects the town*

streets of gabled houses to remind them of home. The chief merchant, who had tried to learn the local language, bargained with the eastern merchants, and kept an eye on the money chest, while others superintended the storehouses and looked after the trading books. Office hours were from six to eleven and one till six, and they worked hard, considering the hot climate.

The Dutch East India Company also employed many skilled Chinese and Malay jewellers, *ebony* furniture makers, dyers, tailors and carpenters. Homes of the traders and officials in the East were full of beautiful furniture and china. Nevertheless, life was rather dull, especially in the evenings when there was little to do except go to the taverns and gossip over a drink and a pipe of tobacco.

Conditions might not have been so bad if there had been more wives in the colonies, but somehow very few respectable Dutch girls seemed to fancy life in the East. They would probably have missed their homely kitchens with their gleaming brass and copper pans and blue-and-white china. So the merchants and officials overseas usually had to content themselves by marrying local Asian girls, after they had been converted to Christianity, or Portuguese girls living there (who were not always very good company). A constant complaint was that they would not learn Dutch—perhaps we cannot blame them — so their husbands had to learn Portuguese, and sometimes also become Catholics to please them.

In fact few people had a good word to say about wives in the East. They were accused of becoming too much like the local people, actually squatting on the floor Eastern fashion instead of using chairs, and eating curry with their fingers, instead of with a spoon. Many of them were very lazy, and spent all their time decking themselves with silk and jewels, while slaves did every job around the house. One newly-wed bride wrote enthusiastically from Batavia to her great-aunt back in Holland that she had fifty slaves in her household. It was almost difficult to decide what to do with them. Apart from the cooks, gardeners, grooms and dressmakers, and a group playing
72 harps, bassoons and viols employed in the slave orchestra

at mealtimes, four or five always stood behind the chairs at table, and a whole queue formed behind the young bride on her journey to church.

All this was fun at first, but soon became rather a bore, and then all there was to do was to gossip with the other merchants' wives, and compare the number of coaches each possessed, and squabble over the seating positions at local banquets. It is hardly surprising that few Dutch peasants could be persuaded to leave their friendly villages, and venture to the unknown East, or that the existing officials hurried home as soon as possible. But even then their poor wives do not seem to have been a great success. They did not always fit in with the more homely life in Holland, put on all kinds of airs, missed their slaves to answer every call, and 'bossed' their servants girls. The latter, used to being treated courteously like one of the family in Holland, were often frank and outspoken, and not slow to give in their notice, and leave their odd employers from overseas.

Yet in spite of all the difficulties, some Dutch merchants and officials obviously enjoyed the colonial life and prospered. On the next page is an illustration of a well-to-do Dutch merchant at Batavia. He has brought his wife from Holland, and they are dressed in respectable European fashions. As these clothes must have been unbearably hot in the tropical climate they were no doubt thankful for the black servant shading them with a broad umbrella. Perhaps they had merely put on their rarely used Sunday best for the portrait, and normally wore cooler clothes. The merchant proudly points with his cane to the source of his prosperity. It is the New Year, and the East Indian fleet is leaving the bay with a cargo of spices on its seven months' voyage to Holland.

THE SETTLEMENT AT THE CAPE
The long haul to the East, lasting several months, made it necessary to organise stopping places where fruit and fresh water could be taken on board. At first the Dutch hoped to use Mozambique in East Africa, but they were unsuccessful in their

attempts to capture it from the Portuguese, so they settled at the Cape of Good Hope.

It did not seem a hospitable area. Table Bay was not a very secure *roadstead*, and offered slight protection for ships from the lashing north gales. There was little timber for building, and few willing local inhabitants to provide a cheap labour force. (There were primitive African Hottentots, and the tiny Bushmen whose descendants still inhabit the Kalahari desert.) The Chinese coolies who, the Dutch hoped, might leave the East and work in South Africa, not surprisingly, were most unwilling to leave their familiar jobs in Batavia.

The new colony owed much to its energetic first governor Jan van Riebeeck who took possession of the country in the name of the Dutch East India Company in 1652. The seventeen Directors discouraged their officials from owning land and farming, but soon free settlers, including groups of girls from Dutch orphanages, came out on the East Indiamen, and the numbers rose to about 600 settlers by the 1670s. Later emigrants were not always Dutch; after Louis XIV persecuted French Protestants, thousands of these came to the Cape bringing their farming skills and enterprise to the colony.

Life in the early settlement was certainly a struggle. Patches of sand and stony ground lay amid the good soil, and farmers usually grew three crops and then had to leave ground *fallow* for a year. Their heavy ploughs, drawn by six to eight oxen, required a team of three men, and everyone, including women and slaves, had to help in getting in the grain at harvest time at Christmas, working hard in the early morning and cool of the evening, and resting from the strong midday heat. Grapes were grown, too, for winemaking, and the French settlers were often quite expert at this. Some farmers kept sheep; mutton was the chief food of the colony, and although the wool was rather poor, the skins could be used for shoe leather.

People on the coast saw more life than those living further

Jan Van Riebeeck, first governor of the Colony at the Cape (Dirck Craey)

inland, since English and French vessels bound for their colon-
76 ies in India also called at the Bay. All who could turned their

homes into 'boarding houses' to accommodate passengers, officials and sailors from the East Indiamen. The visitors usually thought that life in Cape Town was somewhat dreary. They remarked that the inhabitants seemed to know little of events in the outside world, did little reading, and spent most of their leisure time playing cards, smoking and drinking. They complained that the local wine was bitter and the local mutton tough. Everything from the outside world was expensive, and brought by passing vessels: Dutch cheese, beer, and luxury clothing, and from the East tea, silks, and Chinese porcelain. Such visitors were usually glad to leave the Cape.

Had they travelled inland they might have found the life of the rural farmers (called Boeren or boers) who kept cattle and sheep with the help of a few Hottentot herdsmen, even more primitive. They led a sturdy, independent life with little contact with Cape Town, except for the occasional ox wagons that rumbled along the poor rutted country roads. Some inhabited low cottages of unbaked clay with wooden shuttered windows (glass was rare) and uneven floors of beaten earth and cow dung. Others lived in flimsy plastered houses, little better than native huts. All had made their own furniture, rough wooden tables, primitive beds, and chairs with backs of calfskin hide.

Yet in spite of early difficulties, the colony at the Cape continued to prosper, and in many ways the Dutch influence remained strongest here. The Dutch, on the whole, were not interested in settlement overseas. For most of them, life in Holland was more attractive; their government was not harsh, there was freedom to worship in many kinds of churches, their standard of living was high, and most of them loved their simple homes and peaceful countryside. They had a colony in America on Manhattan Island and near the Hudson river called New Netherland which lasted about forty years, but although the climate and countryside were pleasant, and conditions not unlike those in Holland, there was no rush of settlers. The colony was captured without much difficulty by the English in 1664, to be renamed New York.

8 *The Dutch and their English Rivals*

English and Dutch people had much in common, especially their love of freedom, their Protestant religion and their interest in the sea. Furthermore they should have been drawn together by the dangerous threat from France. Yet they competed so strongly against each other that they fought three bitter wars in the mid seventeenth century which caused great hardship and lasting damage to both.

REASONS FOR ENMITY

Much of the trouble arose from quarrels over colonies and trade. Both countries had settlements in eastern America, and trading bases in West Africa and in India, and local skirmishes developed here. The English were anxious for a share in the rich trade of the Spice Islands. When, however, their merchants arrived to trade there, they were driven off by the Dutch, and in a dispute at Amboina, one of the smaller islands, in 1623, several English merchants were killed. Efforts to obtain money from the Dutch to help their widows and orphans came to nothing, and the affair caused much bitterness in England. Englishmen had little sympathy with Dutchmen like the writer Grotius, who urged for freedom to sail the seas. They complained that the Dutch wanted freedom of the seas for themselves alone, and kept the waters around the Spice Islands in the East closed to foreigners.

There were also quarrels over herring fishing in the North Sea. Many Dutch families depended on such fishing for a livelihood, and grew prosperous from the pickled and salted herrings which were sold in many Catholic countries. English

Arctic adventure. Dutch sailors are fighting with Eskimos and polar bears

and Dutch fishermen used to sail to the same fishing grounds, and blows were frequently exchanged. The same thing happened in the whaling grounds around the coast of Greenland. Whaling was a dangerous trade. Every April and May *convoys* of large stout ships, with experienced, hardy crews of 60 to 90 men sailed northwards. They returned by mid August before the ice formed. Whalers carried a great variety of tackle for killing whales, and boilers for extracting oil from their *blubber*. They had five or six smaller whaleboats, each with its helmsman, *harpooner* and four oarsmen. They also carried strong guns to protect them against pirates and rival traders.

Many Dutch boats were well designed, swift and safe, and carried goods for other countries. They delivered promptly, and charged low rates. The English government, jealous of the Dutch carrying trade, passed a Navigation Act in 1651 to prevent English people from using Dutch boats. By the Act all goods sent to England were to be carried in English boats or those of the country they came from, not in ships of a third party, that is the Dutch. It merely annoyed the Dutch further. 79

The English also claimed lordship over the English Channel and the seas around England, and expected other vessels to lower their flags and topsails when meeting English ships, as a mark of respect. Vice-admirals must be hailed with a seven-gun salute, and admirals with a salute of nine guns. Dutchmen, in particular, resented these English claims, and Tromp, the great Dutch admiral, once remarked that he only gave a salute when he met a force of English ships much stronger than his own.

By the mid seventeenth century, although sensible people in both countries regretted the growing *tension*, it had become obvious that both sides would have to fight it out. As a simple English sailor put it: 'The trade of the world is too little for us two; one must down.'

THE TWO SIDES

The English started with several advantages over the Dutch. Their navy had recently been increased in size, and their ships were bigger and had better guns. Robert Blake made various improvements. There was stricter discipline on board, *chaplains* provided regular services, there was increased pay for the men, better arrangements for the sick and wounded, and more efficient signalling. The English also had a superior geographical position. All Dutch cargo ships could be attacked by the English as they passed through the Channel and the North Sea. Moreover war, which took ships and men away from trading, caused greater hardship to the Dutch who depended on their whaling, carrying trade and herring fishing. The English got their livelihood much more from farming and industry. Also since the death of William II of Orange from smallpox in 1650, the Dutch lacked a strong leader, and there was much quarrelling among the seven provinces over who should control the navy, and how the war should be run.

The three wars between Holland and England each lasted two years, after which time both countries were exhausted and glad to make peace. Usually 80 to 100 ships put to sea.

It was not easy to man them. The English press gangs forced

Cornelius Tromp, a great sailor like Martin his father (Peter Lely)

sturdy youths in the ports to join up. The Dutch relied on
volunteers but had to prohibit whaling and herring expeditions

in wartime to secure the necessary sailors. A battle was often confused; both side might claim a victory. Admirals aimed to capture enemy vessels intact as prizes, or lure them onto dangerous sandbanks, or burn them with floating fireships, or destroy them with cannon fire.

In thick fog drums were beaten and trumpets blown to keep the boats in touch with each other. Shortage of gunpowder prevented lengthy battles, and beer and victuals were often scarce. Ships also had to return to shore after a few weeks to be regularly *careened*, or they lost speed and efficiency. The English leaders, Blake, Prince Rupert, Monck and Montagu, Earl of Sandwich were well-to-do soldiers who had turned sailor. The Dutch commanders, Martin Tromp, his son Cornelius, and Michael De Ruyter were humble men who had risen from the ranks to high command and had years of practical experience at sea. Though the wars were fought bitterly and fiercely, each side had a deep respect for the courage and stubbornness of the enemy.

TROMP AND DE RUYTER

Martin Tromp, Dutch leader in the first war (1652–54) had been to sea with his sailor father since he was nine years old, and had had many exciting adventures, capturing Spanish treasure ships and being himself seized by *Barbary* pirates. He respected the English and had served for two years as a cabin boy on an English pirate ship. Later his ship had escorted the English Queen Henrietta Maria with her daughter Princess Mary after she had married William II, Prince of Orange. For this service the English King Charles I personally knighted Tromp in Dover castle.

Tromp was a man of energy, courage, and strong yet simple religious faith. He loved his country deeply and was determined that Holland should not give way to England. The story that he nailed a broomstick to his mast to sweep the English from the seas may not be true, but it is the sort of thing he might have done. In the war, while escorting valuable cargo ships through the Channel, he won a great victory over Blake at

Dus rust dien grooten Tromp die Spangiens gansche Macht
In tien iaar toe gherust in Duyns te gronde Bracht
En SCHEV'LINGH sagh voortlaast de Britse vloot Verplet
Had tnoot lot syne Doot maar enen dach Verset

A model of Martin Tromp's tomb in Delft

Dungeness, but had the worst of the encounter in a second fight at Portland. It was a great loss to the Dutch when he was shot in an action off the Dutch coast towards the end of the war. He was buried with great pomp in the church at Delft, De Ruyter acting as one of his coffin bearers.

The Dutch by this time were almost desperate. They had suffered heavy casualties. Admirals sent urgent reports back to the government that they needed heavier guns and more ammunition, and faster transport ships to replenish their beer and water. The English harried the Dutch coast and interfered with Dutch trading. There was no herring fishing or Greenland whaling, many people were starving with the interruption of corn supplies from the Baltic. It was said that grass was growing in the deserted streets of Amsterdam. So peace was signed in 1654 at Westminster, but it settled none of the main causes of dispute.

Michael De Ruyter fought in all the Dutch wars, and was probably the greatest of all Dutch admirals. He came of a seafaring family from Flushing in Zeeland, and was an intelligent, 83 lively and adventurous lad, although he had little interest in school. As a boy he worked in a ropeyard for sixpence a week, and later sailed in many kinds of ships on the dangerous whaling voyages to Greenland, to the Dutch colony of Brazil (captured for a short time from the Portuguese), to the West Indies and to the Barbary coast of Africa. He carried a variety of cargoes – tobacco, gunpowder, cotton, ginger, pepper and muskets. He traded with Arab rulers of North Africa and rescued Christian slaves they had captured. Legends of his exploits abounded. In one he got the better of Irish pirates by spreading the deck of his ship with cheap Irish butter, and his crew fought in their stockinged feet nimbly against the bewildered pirates who slithered on the slippery surface.

De Ruyter was a heavily built man, with a strong head and shoulders, black hair and moustache, and quiet, kindly eyes. Long years at sea gave him a red weather-beaten complexion. He commanded the deep respect and loyalty of all his sailors. William Temple met him at the height of his fame when he was a wealthy admiral, with a fine house in Amsterdam full of valuable pictures, furniture and Eastern porcelain. Yet he lived modestly. Temple noticed that he wore clothes in the style of the commonest sea captain, travelled on foot and not by carriage, and was never followed by more than one servant. Though great and famous, he lived a simple life with his family, who ate little and drank less. He kept strict account of his money, investing carefully in whaling and profitable trading. On Sundays, and sometimes on weekdays too, he attended church, singing the psalms lustily in a loud voice. He gave generously to the church poor box as a thanksgiving every time he returned home safely after a voyage. Modest and humble on land, at sea De Ruyter took complete command. He dealt with his men strictly but fairly and had their welfare always at heart. He stocked his ships with lemons to improve their health, the wounded were well cared for, and there was always a chaplain on board. Outspoken, and critical of *inefficiency*, De Ruyter could make firm decisions, as hot-tempered and unruly young officers like Tromp's son Cornelius soon found.

Michael De Ruyter, probably the greatest of all Dutch admirals (H. Berckman)

9 Holland and England in War and Peace

The Second Dutch war (1665–67) was largely brought about by troubles in the colonies. In 1664 the English tried to seize the Dutch colony in West Africa, a useful slave trading base, but were prevented by De Ruyter. He regained the Dutch forts and captured valuable stores, including 1400 elephant tusks and 1000 copper cauldrons from the neighbouring English colony of Sierra Leone.

The same year the English attacked the Dutch colony of New Netherland in America. Some thirty years earlier Dutch people had settled on Manhattan island and around the Hudson and Delaware rivers. Few Dutchmen, however, took much interest in the colony and only about 1500 people had emigrated there. Nevertheless from their neighbouring colonies of Virginia and New England the English viewed the Dutch with suspicion, although there was plenty of room for both English and Dutch in the area.

Among the few alive to the danger from England was the enterprising governor of New Netherland, Pieter Stuyvesant. Tough, energetic and obstinate, he thought little of difficulties. His familiar figure with wooden leg decorated with silver bands (he had his right leg amputated after a desperate fight in the West Indies) could frequently be seen stumping round the colony. Stuyvesant tried to introduce reforms. He trained the home guard, stopped drunkenness and brawling (he was deeply religious) and fought against the Indians. Time and again he warned the unheeding Dutch government of the danger of an English attack. In 1664 it came. Disregarding Dutch rights,

Dutch flagships close inshore

Charles II, the English king, granted all lands in the region to his brother the Duke of York, and the English invaded the colony. Stuyvesant's few hundred defenders were no match for the 2000 English soldiers and he was forced to surrender. However the English terms were generous, and the Dutch settlers accepted English rule. Even Pieter Stuyvesant spent the rest of his days happily in the colony, now renamed New York after the King's brother.

The Dutch made determined preparations for the second Dutch war. Throughout the winter of 1665 there were monthly days of fasting and prayer. Old ships were repaired and new ones built. Captains filled their holds with beer, water, food and firewood. The decks were sprinkled with vinegar, and juniper berries burnt as a precaution against the plague. De Ruyter had a new flagship, the 'Seven Provinces', equipped with 80 guns. It could carry over 400 men, and drums were beaten every day along the Dutch coast to enlist recruits.

In May the fleet assembled at Texel Island. It was a gay occasion, and one bold sailor even climbed to the top of one of the main masts and stood on his head in sheer excitement. Amid the thunder of guns the ships were inspected by the fifteen-year-old Prince of Orange. A splendid banquet was held for De Ruyter and his captains, and silver coins and ale distributed to the men. The finest Dutch fleet that had ever set sail put to sea.

The English fleet, organised by the Duke of York, although smaller, was prepared for battle and strongly attacked the Dutch off the English coast at Lowestoft. The next year, in 1666, the ferocious battle of Four Days in June was fought. Thousands of casualties were suffered by both sides. The Dutch lost four ships, the English twelve, and another eight captured, one with its admiral Ayscue aboard. He was imprisoned in a Dutch castle till the end of the war and was said to have been the only English admiral ever to have been captured in a sea fight. The remaining English ships crept home under cover of a thick fog.

Characteristically, De Ruyter remained unmoved by his success, and after the battle he swept out his cabin as usual, and then went to feed his chickens. But he was the hero of Holland. Medals were struck in his honour, and poems written in praise of 'the pillar of the Fatherland'. The rejoicings were shortlived. A few weeks later the English inflicted heavy losses on the Dutch in another bitter battle. De Ruyter's beautiful new flagship suffered great damage and his best admiral was killed. Shortly afterwards in a daring raid on islands along the Dutch coast the English burnt 150 merchant ships of the Dutch East India Company, and destroyed many warehouses of valuable stores.

De Ruyter himself was laid low with a severe fever, and unable to go to sea for months.

In 1667 moves were made towards peace, and the Dutch statesman De Witt decided on a daring plan to speed them up. English spirits were low. The country had recently suffered from a severe outbreak of plague, and Londoners were also recovering from the terrible fire which had destroyed St Paul's cathedral and hundreds of homes. Most of the English ships were in dock in the Thames and Medway, though to protect them halfhearted defences had been prepared. A fort at Sheerness was armed and a heavy iron chain put across the mouth of the river Medway. De Ruyter had secret instructions to sail up the Thames and Medway, and inflict heavy damage on ships and stores.

The stern of the English Flagship, The Royal Charles

It was a dangerous undertaking. The Dutch were unfamiliar with the rivers, and their large ships might be grounded in shallow water. English squadrons in the channel might cut off their rear. But the plan succeeded beyond all expectation. The unprepared garrison in the fort at Sheerness were quickly overwhelmed by a raiding party of Dutch sailors and much booty, guns, masts, pitch and tar captured. Warehouses and stores were soon ablaze and many large warships sunk or burnt. The crowning insult was when the Duke of York's prized flagship, 'The Royal Charles', was captured by the Dutch (the few English crew aboard swam hastily ashore). It was taken to Holland, amid general rejoicing, and its splendid stern remains in Amsterdam to this day. Panic swept through England, and peace was soon signed at Breda.

Shortly after this Temple had his greatest triumph, and the treaty of friendship with Holland was signed in 1668. Temple was anxious that the two countries should work together, and he looked forward, as the new English ambassador in Holland, to many years of close friendliness. But it was not to be. It was soon obvious that Charles II and his chief ministers did not want to be friends with the Dutch, and Temple reluctantly returned home. He would have been angry and ashamed had he known that Charles II had secretly signed a paper with France at Dover agreeing that the two countries would shortly attack Holland. The unsuspecting Dutch still imagined that the English were their friends.

The third war against England broke out in 1672 and was the most disastrous for Holland. The French attacked by land and the English by sea. Soon most of the provinces were overrun by French troops, and Amsterdam threatened. A brutal and starving mob at The Hague turned against the Dutch statesman John De Witt and his brother Cornelius, and in panic and revenge murdered them in the street. It was one of the ugliest moments in Dutch history.

Soon, however, the country recovered. Amsterdam was saved from attack by flooding the surrounding countryside, and the Dutch rallied behind young William of Orange, cool,

John De Witt, the great 17th century Dutch statesman (J. de Baen)

determined, and a great soldier. De Ruyter was as courageous
as ever, winning a great battle off the English coast at South-   91

wold, and dying bravely while fighting in the Mediterranean. England made peace at Westminster in 1674, and France four years later.

PEACEFUL LINKS BETWEEN ENGLAND AND HOLLAND

War between England and Holland lasted for only short periods. During most of the seventeenth century there were close and friendly relations between the two countries. Cargo ships with English cloth and corn, and Dutch tiles and bricks sailed regularly between Amsterdam and Rotterdam in Holland and Hull and King's Lynn. Many English students studied medicine at Leyden university. Hundreds of Scottish seamen and traders lived for years in Dutch cities, and Dutch merchants, artists and craftsmen, especially cloth weavers, settled in London, Norwich, Canterbury and other towns. Individuals, and groups of English people, including the royal family, went to Holland, too, when there was trouble and civil war. Earlier in the seventeenth century some English refugees in Leyden and Amsterdam who had fled from persecution at home even found that their children were growing up too happily as little Dutchmen! So, better known as the Pilgrim Fathers, they set sail in the 'Mayflower' to found an English colony in America.

In eastern England many gabled houses (some still standing) were built in the Dutch style, and enterprising farmers imported Frisian cows and grew turnips, introduced from Holland. Some laid out gardens in the Dutch manner and joined in the craze for tulip-growing. Englishmen admired great Dutchmen like Leevenhoek, the biologist who developed the *microscope*, and the king made him a Fellow of the Royal Society. Many of the books read in England were printed in Amsterdam, and English sailors certainly relied on Dutch maps and charts.

The most important artists in seventeenth-century England, too, came from the Netherlands, and Peter Lely (whose portrait of Temple is on p. 2) was trained in Haarlem, later becoming an English citizen and the Court Painter. Charles II and the Duke of York admired the seascapes of the Van de Veldes who

92

A wedding portrait of William II (aged 14) and Mary his English bride (aged 10)
(Van Dyck)

93

settled in London. In eastern England, especially, artists were greatly influenced by the Dutch landscape painters.

Nowhere was the Dutch influence stronger than in the *fenlands* of Cambridgeshire and Lincolnshire. The 'fennymen' were a hardy and lonely people, travelling from their rough cottages in the higher ground on stilts, or by boat across the flooded swamps, snaring wildfowl, eels and fish. The weird *vapours* of escaping marsh gas made them believe in 'will o' the wisps' and strange spirits, and they warded off the fever of the damp marshes with magical charms. Enterprising landowners like the Duke of Bedford and the king himself had visions of fertile well-drained fields, and turned to the Dutch, experienced in such matters, to help with the fen drainage. In spite of setbacks, Cornelius Vermuyden and his Dutch and English 'Adventurers' worked for many years to cut channels and build windmills, and much was achieved. Records of his carefully planned schemes survive, and modern engineers who have completed the drainage of the fens have shown that his ideas were sound.

There were links, too, between the English royal family and the Princes of Orange. At the age of fourteen William II was married to Princess Mary of England, then only ten. Their son William III became a frequent visitor to Temple's home at The Hague, and supped there twice a week. Temple admired the Prince's good sense, simple tastes and ability. He relates how William asked his advice about marrying since 'he might not be very easy for a wife to live with'. Would Mary, daughter of the Duke of York and niece of Charles II, consent to marry him? Lady Temple had the delicate task of visiting Mary in England and seeing if she were willing. All went well. William came to England, Charles II gave his permission, and the pair were happily wed. Later, in 1688 the links between England and Holland became closer still. William and Mary became King and Queen of England and, for a time, the two countries were under one ruler.

10 The Golden Age and its Decline

Why were the Dutch so prosperous in the seventeenth century? This question intrigued Sir William Temple and many other foreigners, and they tried to find the answer. Temple marvelled at the number of ships built in Holland, though most of the wood, iron, pitch, hemp and flax needed to build them and to make their sails had to be brought from abroad. The Dutch seemed to produce little themselves except butter, cheese and earthenware pottery, yet their country was the centre of European trade. Amsterdam was one of the greatest ports in Europe, but it could only be reached with difficulty by passing Texel Island, and sailing across the Zuider Zee which had treacherous currents, and could be choppy and dangerous at times. Why, in spite of difficulties such as these, were the Dutch so successful?

THE PEOPLE

Dutchmen were hardworking, energetic and *thrifty*. Every encouragement was given to enterprising foreigners, ill-treated in their own country, to settle in Holland. Temple thought that wars, calamities and discontent in neighbouring lands like France and Germany encouraged people to come to Holland 'like birds migrating during a rough winter season fly to some tender and softer climate'. Amsterdam, in particular, welcomed refugees of all kinds: Jews, French Protestants ill-treated by Louis XIV, and craftsmen fleeing from Spanish rule in the south. Workers in the many towns began to specialise in different industries – Haarlem in manufacturing linens and in bulb growing, Delft in making beer and pottery, Gouda in producing clay pipes and cheese.

There was little snobbery and difference between classes as in many other countries. The women were free and independent, taking a great pride in the neatness of their homes; the servants were outspoken and frank, ready to regard themselves almost as the equal of their masters. Quite humble people had a good schooling, and could read, write well, and add up accounts. Also Dutchmen could rise by their hard work and ability to high positions. No one was ashamed of having earned his profits from trading in commonplace things like whale oil or herrings. Nearly everyone was very economical and careful too. 'Men abandon their clothes only because they are worn out, and not because they are out of fashion.' Many Dutch people were very hardworking and went to enormous trouble. Temple had met a man who had spent thirty years *inlaying* a beautiful table with different pieces of wood, and another who had passed twenty-four years making a perfect globe of the world. Undoubtedly these were exceptional craftsmen, but many spent years painstakingly constructing *microscopes*

A beautifully carved Dutch ship's lantern of gilded wood

(developed by a Dutchman in the seventeenth century) and telescopes, or carefully polishing lenses.

There was much care, too, for the aged in old people's homes, and orphanages were set up for poor children. Whereas beggars thronged the streets in many European cities, foreigners were amazed to see so few in Holland.

THE ATMOSPHERE

On his first visit to Holland with his sister Martha, Temple had been struck by 'the strange freedom that all men took of talking openly whatever they thought upon all public affairs'. There was a wonderful liberty and ease, 'every man following his own way, minding his own business and little enquiring into other men's'. Holland became a haven of refuge for thinkers, writers and craftsmen from many lands.

Most Dutch people belonged to a simple Protestant Church called the Dutch Reformed Church. Its teaching and services were based on those of the Church set up in Geneva by a Frenchman called John Calvin. The people were encouraged to read their Bibles regularly, to lead strict, honest lives, and to contribute generously to the schools, orphanages and poor-houses run by the clergy. However there were many other religious groups too: Roman Catholics, Jews, Quakers, even a few Muslims. They were allowed to worship with much greater freedom than in many other countries. This *toleration* was unique in Europe.

THE GOVERNMENT AND MONEY MATTERS

The government, too, was generally fair and just. Each of the seven provinces largely ran its own affairs, and there was a Parliament, called the States General, which met at The Hague to deal with important matters affecting all the states; foreign trade and wars, for example. The province of Holland tended to control the parliament as it was the wealthiest and most important state, and contained Amsterdam, the largest and richest city. Soon the name Holland would be given to the whole country. However, the people in Zeeland, Friesland and 97 other states had their say too.

Usually the wealthy merchants ran the country (and ruled well and sensibly in return for small salaries) but in times of crisis, people tended to rally to the Orange family. As we have seen, they turned to William of Orange as their leader in the seventeenth century, as they had turned to his famous ancestor, William the Silent, who helped them to win their freedom from Spain a century earlier.

Dutch success in money matters, too, was the envy of many foreigners. Temple noted that the English king Charles II had to pay at least 6 per cent in *interest* when he wanted to borrow money. The Dutch government was so sound and respected that it could borrow money easily at $2\frac{1}{2}$ per cent. The wealth of Holland was shared among many people and helped the Dutch to pay for their navy, hire their soldiers, often from abroad, and develop their trading bases overseas. Temple particularly admired the Bank of Amsterdam where people could safely deposit their money. 'The use of banks secures money, and makes all payments easy, and trade quick.' The money, in bars of gold and silver, and large bags of coin, was stored in a great vault under the Town Hall. The amount kept was something of a mystery to Temple, but he was nevertheless greatly impressed by Amsterdam's position as the banking centre of Europe.

DUTCH TRADE

Above all it was her trade that made Holland prosperous. One Dutchman proudly remarked: 'Through our thrifty and shrewd management we have sailed all nations off the seas, drawn almost all trade from other lands here, and served the whole of Europe with our ships.'

The Dutch carried many goods thoughout Europe. They had several boats designed to carry different cargoes, a particularly useful boat being the fly boat or fluit, cheap to sail, with few sailors, and able to carry bulky cargoes. Dutch cargoes were well packed, carefully insured, delivered promptly at low cost. This encouraged other countries to send their goods in Dutch boats. Dutchmen transported three-quarters of the

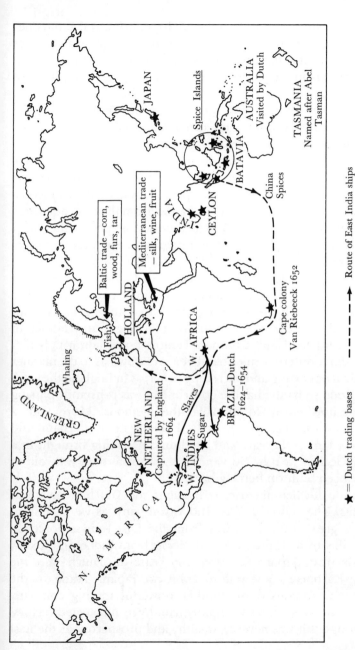

Baltic trade—corn, wood, furs, tar

Mediterranean trade —silk, wine, fruit

GREENLAND

Whaling

N. AMERICA

NEW NETHERLAND
Captured by England 1664

Fish

HOLLAND

Slaves

W. INDIES
Sugar

W. AFRICA

BRAZIL—Dutch 1624-1654

Cape colony
Van Riebeeck 1652

INDIA

CEYLON

JAPAN

Spice Islands

China
Spices

BATAVIA

AUSTRALIA
Visited by Dutch

TASMANIA
Named after Abel
Tasman

★ = Dutch trading bases   – – – ▶ = Route of East India ships

Dutch Trade in the 17th Century

grain and timber from Scandinavian countries, and about one-third of the Swedish minerals. This meant that naval supplies (tar, hemp and flax for canvas, and timber for shipbuilding) were largely in the hands of the Dutch, to the growing alarm of the English.

In return for shipping these things the Dutch sent to the Baltic countries cloth, and dried fruit and wines from the Mediterranean. They went to tremendous lengths to protect their trade. Ships voyaging from distant lands travelled safely together in convoys and the Dutch navy was active in its efforts to reduce pirates who preyed upon ships from their hideouts in Tunis and Algiers, or in the Channel from their headquarters at Dunkirk. Inland, too, Dutch trade was helped by the cheap transport of goods along the numerous waterways by strings of barges.

Herrings (much eaten, especially in Catholic countries in southern Europe on fast days and during Lent) were another source of Dutch wealth. They were cured and packed in salt, which the Dutch had traded from Portugal and France in barrels made of Baltic timber. Temple noted admiringly that over thirty different rules had been laid down as to the manner of curing, pickling and barrelling, whereas in England the work was done so badly that the government was constantly passing regulations trying to improve the methods. More than a thousand fishing smacks left Enkhuizen, Rotterdam and Amsterdam each year, and the humble herring brought in a great deal of wealth. No wonder that Amsterdam was said to have been built on herring bones!

Trade further afield also brought the Dutch tremendous profits. The powerful East India Company, as we have seen, did a great trade in spices from the East Indies, porcelain and silks from China, tea and *calicoes* from India, and luxury goods from Japan. For over 200 years the Dutch were the only Europeans allowed to trade in Japan. Trade in the west was organised by another powerful trading company called the West India Company, run by its nineteen directors. Although this was never as wealthy and prosperous as the East

India Company, many of its merchants made fortunes carrying slaves from Africa to the New World, or in transporting sugar from plantations in Brazil back to Europe.

THE DECLINE OF THE GOLDEN AGE

Towards the end of the seventeenth century Holland began to decline. The change came gradually, and many people remained prosperous, but the Dutch had lost their special position in Europe.

The Dutch population did not increase as fast as that of many other European countries, and a number of towns, including Haarlem, Leyden and Delft, were affected. The Dutch did not

A tin plate with inscription left in Australia in 1616 by Dirk Hartog as evidence that he was the first European on Australian soil

A family making music. Clothes were becoming more extravagant in the later 17th century (Molenar)

develop new industries, and whaling, and cod and herring fisheries were becoming less important. People in the eighteenth century ate fewer herrings, and countries like England and France were developing their own fleets. With the decline of fishing, shipbuilding, carpentry, rope and net-making also suffered. Neighbouring countries, France and England especially, put heavy duties on Dutch goods entering their ports, and discouraged their people from buying Dutch products. Dutch people had to pay heavy taxes on everyday things like bread, meat, salt and paper to pay for their wars, and this led to demands for high wages. This often meant that their goods were more expensive to produce than those of their neighbours. Three devastating wars against England, and invasion by France towards the end of the seventeenth century were probably the chief reasons why the Dutch lost power and wealth. They had fewer people and less money to govern their colonies successfully, although they kept the Cape till 1815, and did not give up the East Indies till the twentieth century.

William Temple retired to England. He refused to accept further government posts, and did not seek power, wealth or court favours. 'I do not know how to ask or why, and this is not an age when anything is given without it.' He had little in common with many of the selfish and ambitious politicians and courtiers in London. He preferred to live quietly in the country, walking, riding and entertaining friends at his Surrey home. He had looked forward to retiring to Sheen, 'and if my life wears not out too soon I may end it in a corner there.'

He wrote many books of essays and poetry, his papers being kept in order by his hardworking secretary Jonathan Swift. He suffered personal sorrows, too; his beautiful fourteen-year-old daughter Diana died of smallpox, and his son John was tragically drowned in the river Thames. However he found contentment in the company of his beloved wife Dorothy, and in cultivating his beautiful garden. Love of his family and of Holland had been the chief interests of his life, but he had also done much for England. When he died in 1695 he was buried in Westminster Abbey. He served his country well.

How Do We Know?

First, there are material remains. A number of seventeenth century houses, including Rembrandt's in Amsterdam, still survive. They have altered little since those days, so we can imagine Dutch homes. Artists also painted many pictures of country scenes and sports, rooms and their furnishings, and portraits of people wearing fashions of the period. Some of these are illustrated in this book. Dutch museums, especially the Rijksmuseum in Amsterdam, and the Frans Hals museum in Haarlem, contain objects such as chairs, models of ships, lanterns and weapons.

From stray 'finds' we know of the voyages of Dutch sailors to isolated places. Not long ago on an island called Nova Zembla off the Arctic coast, the Russians uncovered a Dutch captain's compasses, log-book, crockery and maps which had been preserved in the ice. There is evidence that the Dutch visited the west coast of Australia because a pewter plate, signed by Dirk Hartog and dated 1616, was recently dug up. In 1963 some divers discovered the remains of a seventeenth century Dutch East Indiaman blown off course, and wrecked off the West Australian coast. Its cargo of ivory elephant tusks, wine bottles, and a rich coin haul of 'pieces of eight' was encrusted with coral, but well preserved.

Secondly, there are accounts written at the time, one of the most detailed being William Temple's 'Observations on the United Provinces'. Merchants in the East Indies wrote letters home describing the scenery, the lives of the natives, and the cargoes they sold there. Captains, like De Ruyter, kept detailed log-books of their voyages and gave accounts of battles at sea. As the Dutch wars with England were also described in English diaries (such as that of Samuel Pepys) we have a vivid picture of events as seen from both sides. We can still read the careful accounts of the draining of the fens by Vermuyden and his 'Adventurers' which are preserved in a little seventeenth-century book in the record office in Cambridge.

Things To Do

1 Start a collection of picture postcards of paintings by Dutch artists (many stationers and art shops stock these). From them you can find out a great deal about seventeenth-century Dutch life. Your art master or mistress may also have books about Dutch art, and pictures by Vermeer, Rembrandt, Frans Hals and Pieter de Hooch can be found in books in your local library.

2 Your local museum may have an original Dutch painting or two, dating from this period. There are fine collections at the National Gallery in London, the Ashmolean Museum in Oxford (mostly pictures of still life) and the Fitzwilliam Museum in Cambridge. You may be able to visit these some time.

3 Through school you could possibly arrange to correspond with a Dutch 'pen friend'. (Many Dutch children can speak English.) You could send pictures of your town or village, and tell each other something about its important people and its history. Sometimes such friendships result in rewarding exchange visits.

4 Find out all you can about presentday Holland and build up a scrapbook. Travel agencies often supply brochures and maps; there are bulb catalogues, and interesting postage stamps.

5 Imagine yourself living in seventeenth-century Holland. Write a diary to describe your food, clothes and everyday life. It could be illustrated with drawings based on the pictures in this book.

6 Do you think seventeenth-century Holland was like England at the same period? If you have read 'Samuel Pepys in London' in this series you might like to compare the two countries.

7 Try to find out if there has been any Dutch influence where you live, e.g. gabled houses, pottery in your local museum, Dutch ships visiting (if you live in a port). If you are unsuccessful in this, work out why there might have been less contact in your area than in some parts of the country.

8 Anyone interested in ships would enjoy reading 'Sailing ships and   105

sailing craft' by George Goldsmith – Carter (Paul Hamlyn, London) This has some fine illustrations of ships of all periods. You can find out more about windmills in a little book called 'Discovering Windmills' by J. N. T. Vince (Shire Publications, 1968), and there are exciting accounts of whaling in 'Moby Dick' by Herman Melville.

Glossary

almshouse, home for the aged poor
apprentice, learner of a craft
astronomy, study of the stars and heavenly bodies
auction, public sale
Barbary, Arab countries in North Africa
blubber, fat of whales
bulbous, swollen like a bulb
Buss, a small two-masted Dutch vessel
calico, cotton cloth (from Calicut, India)
to careen, to clean a ship turned on its side
carrack, large cargo ship, originally Portuguese
to caulk, to stop up the seams of a ship with oakum and melted pitch
causeway, paved highway
chaplain, priest on board ship
clog, wooden shoe
coat of arms, heraldic design on a shield, showing the family's status
convoy, fleet of ships under escort
cordwainer, leather worker or shoemaker
damask, material of silk, linen or wool, with a woven pattern
decorous, seemly, appropriate
defective, faulty
democratic, rule by the people
diplomat, someone skilled in relations with other countries
dissection, cutting up a plant or body to see how it is made
dyke, embankment to prevent flooding
ebony, hard, black wood
to enhance, to increase in value or importance
etching, copy taken from a drawing on a copper plate
fallow, ploughed land left uncultivated
fenland, marsh land
gable, triangular-topped end wall of a building
guild, group of craftsmen practising the same craft
harpooner, one who throws a barbed dart or *harpoon* when whaling   107

harpsichord, keyboard instrument, forerunner of the piano

hourglass, glass measure through which sand ran in one hour, early time-keeper.

illiterate, unable to read or write

imbecile, person weak in mind

inefficient, not fully capable

to inlay, to fit something into the surface of another

interest, money paid for the use of a sum lent

journeyman, trained craftsman

kermis, a fair

luscious, very sweet

lute, stringed musical instrument

luxuriantly, richly, abundantly

margrove, a tropical tree which grows on muddy shores and river banks

microscope, a powerful lens for magnifying small things

moderation, the avoiding of extremes

navigation, the art of direction keeping at sea or in the air

patron, influential person giving financial support to another

pewter, grey metal made of tin and lead

plebeian, of low birth, vulgar

porcelain, fine earthenware, china

predikant, a minister of the Dutch Reformed Church

press gang, group of officials who pressed (compelled) men for service in the navy

prestige, reputation, influence

roadstead, place where ships can safely lie at anchor near the shore

ruff, circular frill worn round the neck

scurvy, disease caused by lack of suitable food

seascape, picture of the sea

silhouette, a figure seen in outline only, usually dark against a light background

still life, painting of objects such as flowers and fruit.

subsoil, soil under the surface.

tension, strained condition of the nerves

textiles, woven fabric

thrifty, not wasteful, economical

toleration, allowing to others freedom of expression, religion etc.

vapour, steamy moisture

to ventilate, to allow fresh air to circulate

versatile, many-sided in talents and interests

108 *viol*, musical instrument with five, six or seven strings.